CONTENTS

Preface

Many mountain bikers are nervous about working on their own bike. It's understandable – modern mountain bikes look pretty complicated. But they only look complicated because nearly all of the moving parts are on show and readily accessible. This makes mending bikes relatively straightforward – you can get at just about everything easily, with a small selection of simple tools.

Our aim with *The Roadside Mountain Bike Maintenance Manual* has been to distill the most useful information and most common jobs into a compact volume that can live in your toolbox or be chucked in the trunk of your car if you head out for a weekend of off-road fun. We've covered the key aspects of mountain bike maintenance here so you'll have all the basic information you need to keep your bike in good shape, make straightforward adjustments and fixes and fix problems that may arise when you are out on the trail.

Every mountain biker should be able to work on his or her own bike, even if it's just the simple things. We hope this book will give you the confidence to do it.

Mike Davis and Guy Andrews

Acknowledgments

Sincerest thanks to all the companies that supplied bikes and equipment to help in the making of this book: Madison (Shimano, Park Tools, Genesis and Ridgeback bikes and a whole pile of other stuff); Trek (bikes and shoes); ATB Sales (Marin and Whyte bikes); DMR (bikes and components); Fisher Outdoor Leisure (SRAM); Cambrian (Continental tires); Silverfish (Race Face, Rock'n'Roll lubes); Chicken & Sons (Mavic, Time, Sapim); Cycling Sports Group (Cannondale).

Special thanks to photographer Gerard Brown – without his patience, experience and attention to detail this book wouldn't have been as well illustrated – and Jonathan Briggs for tireless layout work (and frequent rejigging thereof).

Guy would like to thank Frank Hornby, the inventor of Meccano, for inspiring him in things mechanical, and his dad, Keith Andrews, who taught him the benefits of both reading and ignoring instruction manuals.

Mike would also like to thank his dad, Bob Davis, from whom he appears to have got a desire for taking things apart (and sometimes putting them back together again). Also Sandra for her deep reserves of patience and encouragement, and Isla and Oscar for reminding him about the simple fun of riding bikes.

Visit a good bike shop and you're likely to be impressed by the workshop facilities – the best shops have spacious, clean and comprehensively equipped workshops that you almost certainly won't be able to replicate at home. The good news is that you don't need to.

YOUR TOOL KIT

Professional workshops need to be able to deal with large numbers of bikes and handle anything that comes through the door. Your home workshop only has to cope with your own bikes, which massively reduces the amount of space and equipment you need. There are also a number of tools that it's generally not worth owning as a home mechanic, and they tend to be the big, expensive ones. A shop might use, say, a frame facing tool several times a week – you might need one once in several years.

The best strategy with tools is to equip yourself with the most basic essentials first, which shouldn't cost too much – you can do a huge amount of work on a bike with just a set of Allen wrenches or a simple multitool. Add extra tools when the need arises – as your confidence builds and you tackle harder jobs, your collection of tools will grow appropriately. This approach spreads out your expenditure on tools and avoids the trap of acquiring expensive but rarely used tools.

BASIC ESSENTIALS

These tools will get you started with simple cleaning and adjustment jobs. If you get nothing else, get these.

- **Allen wrenches – 1.5,2,2.5,3,4,5,6,8 and 10mm are the sizes most often used**
- **Floor pump**
- **Chain cleaner**
- **Cleaning brushes**
- **Pliers (flat and needle nose)**
- **Cable cutters**
- **Screwdrivers (small and large; flat and cross-head)**

We'd always recommend buying high-quality tools. They may cost a little more, but good tools last for years. Trying to undo stubborn bolts with cheap, soft Allen wrenches is frustrating and likely to end up with you damaging something on your bike or yourself. Specialist bike

COMPREHENSIVE HOME TOOL KIT

As you progress to replacing parts, you'll need to extend your tool kit. These are tools to get as you need them.

- **Nylon hammer (or mallet) and ball-peen (metal-working) hammer**
- **Metric, open-ended wrenches – 8 and 10mm cover most jobs but it may make more sense to buy a full set**
- **Cassette lock ring tool**
- **Chain whip**
- **Cable puller**
- **A sharp-ended tool like an awl**
- **Star nut-setting tool**
- **Adjustable wrench**
- **Cone wrenches (17mm, 15mm and 13mm)**
- **Pedal wrench**
- **Workshop-quality chain tool**
- **Chain checker (for measuring chain wear)**
- **Torque wrenches**
- **Crank-removing tool**
- **Bottom bracket tools**
- **Headset wrenches (if you have an old bike)**
- **Spoke wrenches**
- **Disc brake bleed kit**
- **Files (flat and half round)**
- **Socket set**

tools are expensive, but they make complicated procedures a breeze. Stumbling through jobs with cheap tools only ends in compromise, and if you have a good-quality bike it deserves the tools to complement it.

THE TOOLS

1 Tool box
2 Long-nose pliers
3 Allen wrenches
4 Chainring bolt wrench
5 Chain tool
6 Screw drivers
7 Chain whip
8 Pedal wrench
9 Cone wrenches
10 Chain wear tool
11 Crank remover
12 Adjustable wrench
13 Cassette tool
14 Cable cutters
15 Tire levers
16 Truing stand
17 Crank bolt wrench
18 Torque wrench
19 Multitool
20 Shimano Bottom Bracket tool
21 Star-fangled nut setter
22 Crank remover
23 Cassette tool
24 Cable puller
25 Wrench
26 Headset wrenches
27 Cable pliers
28 Soft mallet

LUBRICANTS AND CLEANERS

You don't need special bike products for all cleaning and lubrication jobs, but it's easier to identify the right stuff that way and they tend to come packaged in more convenient quantities.

- Ti prep (or "copper slip") – a grease with tiny copper flakes in it, which prevents titanium and alloys from seizing; this must be used on all titanium threads.
- Anti-seize grease – this is for large threads and components that stay put for long periods (seatposts, bottom bracket threads, headset cups and pedal threads).
- PTFE (Teflon)-based light dry lube – this is preferred for summer use and assemblies like derailleurs and brake caliper pivots.
- Heavy wet lube – this is best for wet weather as it's harder to wash away than dry lube.
- Silicone grease – use these for intricate moving parts like pedal and hub bearings.
- Waterproof grease – use these for components that get ignored for long periods like headset bearings.
- Degreaser – used for cleaning moving parts and components that get mucked up.
- Bike wash – this speaks for itself; use it for tires, frame tubes and saddles.
- Release agent – this is good for removing seized seatposts and stubborn bottom brackets. Be careful as it can ruin your paint, and your skin.

A SELECTION OF LUBES AND GREASES – SEVERAL ARE NEEDED FOR DIFFERENT MATERIAL APPLICATIONS

02 CHECKING AND CLEANING

It's often said that an ounce of prevention is better than a pound of cure, and that's very true of bike maintenance. Keeping a careful eye on your bike means that you're more likely to spot any imminent component failures before they happen. That lets you tackle them at home with access to proper tools, rather than trying to work your way out of trouble on a windswept hillside.

PRE-RIDE SAFETY CHECKS

There are a number of important, but quick, checks to make before each ride. The best pre-ride safety measure is to wash your bike after every ride (see pages 14-17). Washing your bike means you get up close to it, so you'll notice damage like cracks and dents and will also be able to inspect the derailleurs, chains and brakes for wear and tear. Always check anything unusual, like noises and creaks.

Here are 12 safety checks that you should always perform before going on a ride.

1 Frame. Frames don't last forever – they can get bent or suffer from metal fatigue and begin to crack. Look out for cracks around the welds, ripples or folds around the head tube and flaking paint, as they are all signs that the tube underneath has been twisted out of shape. If your bike has a steel frame, be aware of rust spots as these can be a sign of further damage on the inside of the frame tubes.

2 Suspension fork. To check the fork action, apply the front brake and give the fork a few pumps – it should feel smooth, not sticky or notchy. Also note the rebound speed – if it is very slow there may be a loss in pressure or a spring failure. If it's extremely fast you may have lost damping oil. See pages 105-109 for more on fork setup and maintenance.

3 Rear shocks and suspension. Make regular inspections of the bearings and pivots. Keep the air pressure in the shock consistent to maintain the ride quality and place less strain on the moving parts. A depressurized shock out on the trail can damage the frame if you have to ride home, so consider taking a shock pump on the ride for emergencies, especially if you are going to be miles from home. See page 108 for more on rear shock set-up.

4 Tire pressure. All types of inner tubes and valves leak air gradually. Some lightweight tubes and tubeless tires can lose as much as 20 per cent of their pressure overnight, so always check your tire pressure. Use a floor pump with an accurate pressure gauge if you can. Make a note of your preferred tire pressure – the recommended range can be found on the tire sidewall. Also inspect the treads for thorns, and glass, which may have become lodged in the tread. See pages 95-104 for more on tires and tubes.

5 Wheels. Spin the wheels to check for smooth, quiet running and to ensure the brakes aren't binding. Grasp the top of each tire and try to rock it side to side – if there's movement then the wheel bearings are likely to need adjustment or replacement. Lots of movement in the rear wheel could also be caused by worn or loose pivots in the rear suspension.

6 Brakes and headset. Disc brakes are self-adjusting, but if the levers come back to the bars the pads are probably worn. If you have rim brakes, check for rim and pad wear visually – the pads have indicator lines in them and this is common on rims too. If your rims wear through they can split, which usually results in a nasty tire blow-out. While you're pulling brakes, rock the bike slightly back and forth with the front brake on – any looseness here suggests that the headset may be loose. See Chapter 5 for more on brakes and pages 110-112 for more on headsets.

7 Handlebars. Make sure that the handlebars are tight and check for bends or scratches. The basic rule is: if it's bent or scratched, trash it. Bends and scratches are both signs of fatigue – a bend will eventually snap and a scratch will act as a stress riser, which, given time and enough abuse, will eventually fail. See pages 64-71 for more on bar and stem setup.

8 Contact points. Contact points are where you rest your hands, feet and backside. They're all load-bearing and can loosen. Check the saddle fixing bolts on seatpost, seatpost binder bolt, pedals, crank bolts, stem and handlebar clamp bolts. Do not over-tighten, as over-stressed nuts and bolts are more likely to fail under impact. Use a torque wrench to check they are tightened to the manufacturers' recommended torque figures. See pages 63-78 for more on contact points.

9 Pedals. If you use SPDs or other clipless pedals, clean out your shoe cleats and retention mechanisms and lubricate the moving parts of the pedal. If it's muddy, spray some Teflon lube onto them to help shed mud. See pages 72-78 for more on pedal care.

10 Chain and cassette. Check the chain and cassette for wear and always apply fresh lube before you ride: wet oil for muddy and wet conditions and a dry Teflon lube for dusty summer trails. Clean the chain regularly too, as it will last far longer and shift better if it's not covered in dirt. Always run through the gears to check that they index properly and make sure all the cables move freely and aren't bent. See chapter 3 for more on gear systems and chapter 4 for more on the drivetrain.

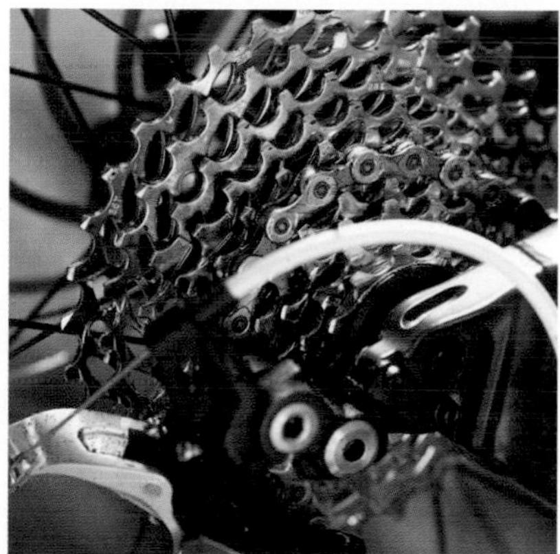

11 Front and rear wheel quick-releases. Check that the front and rear wheel quick-release mechanisms are tight. If you arrive at the trail head in a car, chances are you will have to put the wheels back on the bike before you start riding, but if you don't it's worth double-checking that they are tight, especially if you use disc brakes. See pages 80-85 for more on removing wheels.

12 Tool kit and spares. Once you're happy that your bike is sound, you're good to go. But don't forget to take your trail tools and spares with you. See chapter 10 for on the trail advice.

CLEANING YOUR BIKE

Find a suitable area to clean your bike. Be aware that you will need plenty of water and that the by-products from a mountain bike can be quite messy. Therefore, a concrete area with a water supply and a drain is best. Always clean the floor with a stiff brush when you have finished as the de-greasing fluids can make the floor very slippery.

1 Start at the top of the bike and work down, so you don't get muck on stuff you have already washed. If you're doing a thorough clean then do the saddle and seatpost before putting the bike into a workstand.

2 Use a big brush and a sponge to get the worst of the mud off the frame and tires. It's a lot easier to remove mud when it's wet, so clean your bike as soon as possible after riding. If you've been to a race or ride in the car, try to find space for a water container to get the worst off before setting off for home.

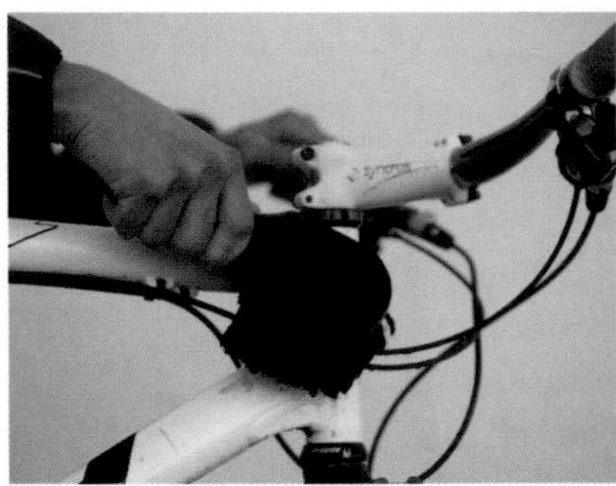

3 Use a spray-on degreaser. You can dilute these cleaning sprays as they tend to be quite concentrated and powerful, and can even go 50:50 with many of them. Be careful to read the instructions as these fluids can be caustic and affect the finish of your bike – generally you don't want to leave them on too long before rinsing off. Most aren't too kind to your hands either, so it's best to wear rubber gloves.

4 You can (and should) use a more powerful degreaser on the chain, chainrings and sprockets. Because these are exposed, lubricated and low on the bike, they tend to get more gunked up than other parts. Removing wheels improves access, but it's easier to degrease the cassette and chain with the wheel in place – just spray the cassette and turn the pedals backward to get the whole chain.

5 Use a small, stiff brush (an old tooth brush is ideal if you don't have a bike-specific one) to clean the chain and sprockets. The idea is to agitate the degreaser so it works more effectively. Then get plenty of fresh water on the brush. Optionally, you can use a chain cleaner (see page 17).

6 Clean stubborn bits of dirt from between cassette sprockets either with a special tool as shown or with any stiff, narrow improvised tool – the edge of a rag or an old spoke works well. Every few cleans take the cassette off completely to clean behind it.

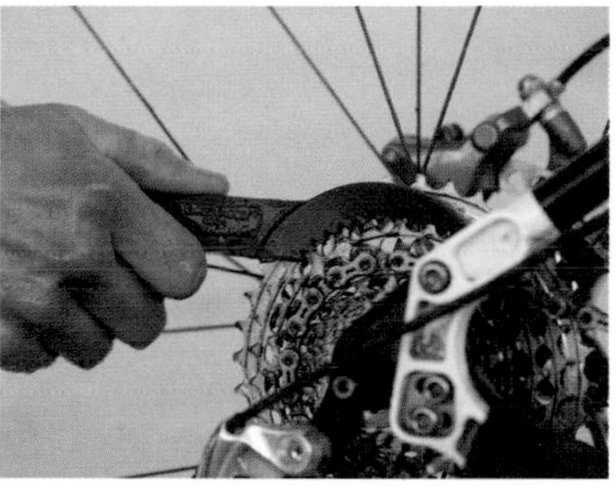

7 Intricate bits like derailleurs and pedals are best tackled with a small, stiff brush that lets you get into all the little corners and gaps. A bottle brush, with bristles all the way around, is effective for the gaps between stays and tires if you've left the wheels on.

8 Take care when cleaning disc brakes. Old chain oil or any kind of lubricant is bad for brake pads, so be careful about which brush you use and get some fresh water. Alcohol-based disc brake cleaning spray is effective.

9 Take similar precautions for suspension forks and shocks. They don't like water inside them, and while most degreasers sold for use on bikes won't harm the seals, it's safest to keep it away from them anyway. Be careful not to scratch stanchion tubes and shock shafts by brushing or wiping grit over them.

10 Finish off by wiping down the frame with a soft cloth, and use a bit of water-displacing lubricant on the chain, sprockets, derailleurs and pedals. Relube the chain when it's dry.

PRO CLEANING TIPS

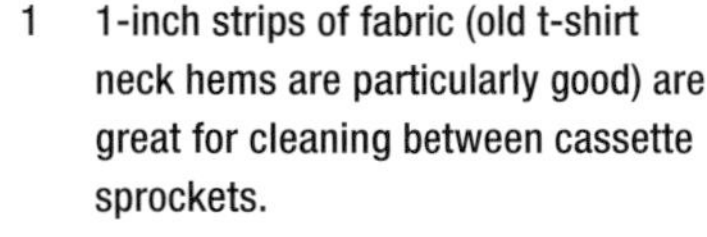
1 1-inch strips of fabric (old t-shirt neck hems are particularly good) are great for cleaning between cassette sprockets.

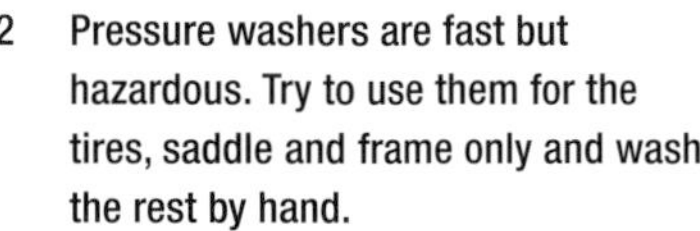
2 Pressure washers are fast but hazardous. Try to use them for the tires, saddle and frame only and wash the rest by hand.

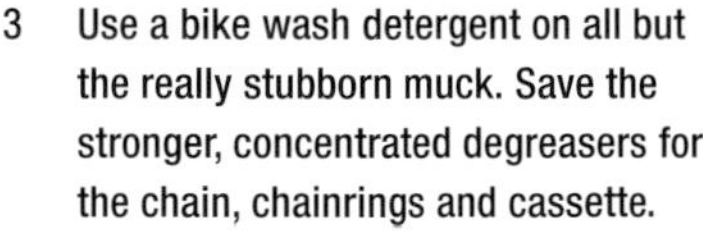
3 Use a bike wash detergent on all but the really stubborn muck. Save the stronger, concentrated degreasers for the chain, chainrings and cassette.

USING A CHAIN CLEANER

While you can get perfectly satisfactory results by cleaning the chain with degreaser, water and a brush, chain bath cleaners are quick, easy and relatively clean.

1 Take the wheels off the bike and place the chain on a chain retainer. This is a device like a dummy axle that positions the chain as if there were a wheel in place.

2 Clean in between the cassette sprockets and get all of the muck out of the jockey wheels on the derailleur. If you don't, the clean chain will get dirty again as soon as you replace the wheels and turn the pedals.

3 Fill the chain bath with a strong mixture of citrus degreaser and water and attach it to the chain. Different brands vary, check the manufacturer's instructions.

4 Hold onto the chain bath and rotate the pedals a few times to get a spotless chain – it's magic! Dispose of the used degreaser appropriately.

LUBRICATING

Lubrication helps prevent corrosion, but leaving a chain dirty and simply re-lubing it will just help attract more dirt. In the long term, this leads to a build-up of gunk and accelerated chain and sprocket wear. The key to proper lubrication is to clean the component before you add any oil. Oiling an already mucky bike will just attract more muck, and cleaning components regularly will keep them running for a long time. Only use bicycle-specific lubricants as some water-repellent sprays and lubricants have solvents in them that can damage the sensitive parts of your bike and ruin your paint.

WHAT LUBRICANT FOR WHERE?

JOCKEY WHEELS

Spraying thick lube all over the jockey wheels just attracts more crud to the chain and rear derailleur. If you have been riding a lot in wet weather, it's worth stripping the derailleur and regreasing the bushings inside the jockey wheels.

CABLES

Inner cables can be stripped out of the slotted cable guides and lubricated with a Teflon-based lubricant. A thin, light lube is best so as not to attract dirt. Many bikes now come with continuous cable housing which leaves fewer places for dirt to creep in.

CHAIN

Clean the chain and use a dry lube in the summer and a wet lube in the winter or in wet weather. Use a water-repellent spray after washing and lube before every ride.

REAR DERAILLEUR

Use a thin lube on the rear derailleur and drop some oil onto the pivots. Work this in by running through the gears a few times. Check the spring inside the derailleur as it should be clean and rust-free.

FRONT DERAILLEUR

The more powerful spring in the front derailleur makes it less prone to sticking but the pivots will benefit from a drop of dry lube squirted and worked into the moving parts. Wipe off any excess with a rag.

BRAKE LEVERS

Like any moving part, brake levers benefit from a squirt of lube to the pivot every now and again. If you're using cable-operated brakes make sure that the cable nipple can move freely in the cable-retaining hole. If this goes dry, the friction can damage the lever or break the cable.

PEDALS

Clipless pedal mechanisms must be cleaned and lubricated regularly. They will clog up quickly if they are permanently dirty, so clean them if you've been riding (and walking) in mud. Clean the cleats in the shoes too as mud can get impacted into the soles and will prevent the cleats from releasing smoothly.

SHIFTERS

It's best not to spray lots of tacky substances into these sensitive components. Lubricate them with a dry lube or light oil occasionally.

SUSPENSION FORKS

Never lubed your forks? Well, you should – a couple of drops of wet lube worked in with a couple of pumps on the bars will keep the seals sweet.

SUSPENSION BIKES

As with the forks, the rear suspension unit needs a drop of oil occasionally. The pivots and bushings also need a squirt of lube, especially after wet rides.

CANTI STUDS

If you're using rim brakes, spray a small amount of light dry oil behind the brake arm and onto the pivot. Obviously, do not spray the rims at the same time! Remove and regrease the studs on a regular basis as they are steel and will rust if exposed to lots of wet weather.

TRACKING DOWN NOISES

Other than a bit of chain clatter, bikes ought to be almost silent. Noises usually mean that something isn't right somewhere, so identifying the source of a noise is a key maintenance skill. Try to narrow down the possibilities – if there's a creaking sound when pedaling, try standing up and sitting down to eliminate the saddle and seatpost as a cause. Try pedaling with one leg at a time. Some noises only appear when pedaling hard, but such noises could come from the bars or stem – you tend to pull on the bars when pedaling. If a noise doesn't go away when you're coasting, it's likely to be wheel-related rather than the transmission. Noises don't always come from where they sound like they do – frames are often good at transmitting sounds and making them appear to be emanating from somewhere else. Always check the simple things first – many noises can be cured just by tightening a loose bolt.

SQUEAKS AND CREAKS

A persistent noise from your bike can drive you mad. Squeaks, ticks and creaks can originate from many different places and they often need a careful process of elimination to find the source of the noise. Noises mean that there is something wrong so take them seriously. Take some time to track them down and sort out whatever it is.

The main cause of noise from your bike will be dry bearing surfaces or loose components. The friction between surfaces, whether at the threads in your bottom bracket or the clamp on your handlebars, will not be solved by spraying copious amounts of penetrating lubricant into the component – and in particular, don't do this to your handlebars as they could slip and cause a nasty accident. You can't always solve the problem simply by turning the bolts a little tighter either, as they have recommended tightening torques and may simply need some anti-seize compound applied to them if they are titanium or aluminum. A persistent tapping can be something as simple as a cable end hitting the cranks as you pedal, or something less obvious like a broken chain roller, a worn freewheel or a loose hub. All the components should be checked for cracks or splits, and anything that looks unusual should be checked out and replaced if necessary.

SADDLE

The saddle is often the cause of pedaling-related noises. As the saddle is usually exposed to the muck from the rear wheel, it gets a lot of abuse and very little cleaning or care. The small shifts in weight across the saddle as you pedal cause movement in the rails, which can wear or start to work loose in the shell. The bolts in the seatpost can creak too. You may need a new saddle, or sometimes just removing it, cleaning everything, regreasing the bolts and re-installing will quieten everything down.

SEATPOST

A dry seatpost will seize up pretty quickly. The residue and corrosion inside the seat tube can make a nasty creaking sound. Remove the seatpost and carefully clean inside the seat tube. Seriously corroded seat tubes will need reaming (cleaning out with a special cutting tool). Clean the seatpost with some wire wool and re-apply anti-seize grease (or assembly paste for a carbon fiber post) before you replace it.

SEATPOST CLAMP

Most frames have a separate seatpost clamp that pushes onto the frame. It needs to be a perfect fit and suitably tight. Seatpost clamps are also right in the line of fire of dirt from the rear wheel and need regular cleaning and regreasing. In particular, pay attention to the cam of quick-release clamps and the bolt in bolt-up clamps.

BOTTOM BRACKET

This is probably the biggest cause of pedaling noise. To solve any problems you'll have to remove it and at least clean and lubricate it. You may need to replace the bearings. See pages 46-54 for more information.

CRANKS

The traditional square-taper bottom bracket is often a cause of creaks and clicks, but that's now only found on old or inexpensive bikes. Most mid- to high-end bikes now use two-piece cranks with the spindle permanently attached to one crank arm – they're less susceptible to noise, but not immune. See pages 46-49 for more on removing and replacing cranks.

CHAINRINGS

Worn chainrings can cause all sorts of problems. As well as not running quietly, worn teeth can let the chain jump which is potentially dangerous. It gets worse with a new chain, too. Check for hooked or missing teeth and replace if necessary. See pages 53-54 for more on chainrings.

CHAINRING BOLTS

These can often dry out and start to click as a result. Remove them, clean the cranks thoroughly and reassemble with anti-seize compound on the bolts.

CHAIN

This is often the cause of drivetrain noises. Stiff links can click or tap and are likely to cause skipping too. A very worn chain will make a raunchy rattling noise no matter how much lube you throw at it. Chain maintenance tips are on page 40-43.

CASSETTE AND CASSETTE BODY

The cassette body is part of the rear hub and contains the freewheel mechanism. They don't last forever – a worn one will rock on the hub and may start to slip or stick. Either way it'll be making a bad noise by then. Flushing with light oil can get a few more miles out of them but it's usually a replacement job. Loose cassette lockrings, or loose screws holding cassettes together, can cause clicking or ticking sounds as well as affecting shifting.

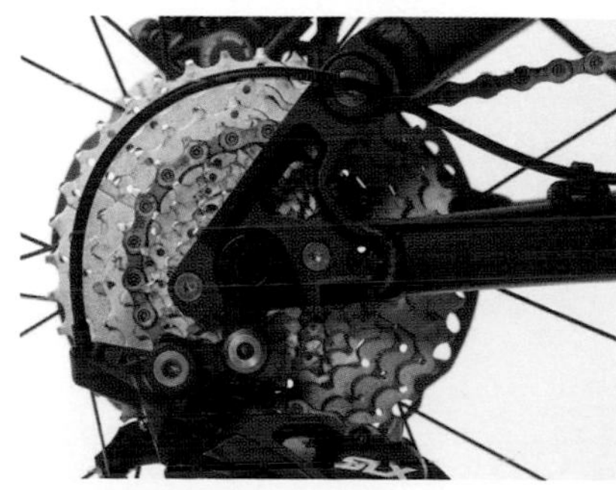

REAR DERAILLEUR

Squeaks are often associated with dry jockey wheel bushings. If the squeak stops when you stop pedaling, it's probably caused by either the pedals, bottom bracket or jockey wheels – these are the parts that rotate when pedaling. Badly adjusted gears will make a whirring or clicking sound – check that the derailleur hanger hasn't been bent and thrown the gears out of line.

FRONT DERAILLEUR

Very worn front derailleurs can rattle, and the sound is often amplified by the frame. Other common issues are clonking from the crank hitting a badly-adjusted derailleur cage or ticking from the crank or your feet tapping a protruding cable end.

HUBS

Traditional cup and cone bearings need regular servicing, while cartridge bearings need periodic replacement. Both tend to deteriorate without you noticing until they get really bad. By the time they start making a noise, they'll be in need of serious attention.

PEDALS

Loose pedal bearings can cause creaks or clicks, while dry threads in the crank arms can cause creaks. Worn shoe cleats can be noisy too, and on some pedals the top plate can wear. Everything can be replaced, and often bearings can be made like new with a strip and regrease.

HANDLEBARS

Handlebar creaks usually emanate from the front stem clamp due to loose or dry bolts. They need to have grease on them and be evenly tightened. But check the bar closely for cracks too – creaks are often the first sign of a broken bar.

STEM

As well as the handlebar clamp, stems have a clamp at the back to attach to the steerer and those can work loose or have dry bolts too. Other possible sources of creaking are the star-fangled nut inside the fork steerer tube or the top cap.

HEADSET

Dry bearings or broken races will make a very unpleasant creak as you pull on the handlebars. A strip and rebuild will usually eliminate the noise – re-pack the bearings with grease if you can, although cartridge bearings will generally need to be replaced. A badly-adjusted headset will produce a knocking sound and a rattle that you can feel when riding. This can usually be adjusted out but if left too long may damage the headset. Very occasionally creaks come from the bearing races pressed onto the fork crown and into the frame. See pages 110-113 for headset adjustments.

SUSPENSION FORK

Many suspension forks make twanging, gasping, or other noises even when in perfect working order, so you're listening for new or different ones. Hissing can be a

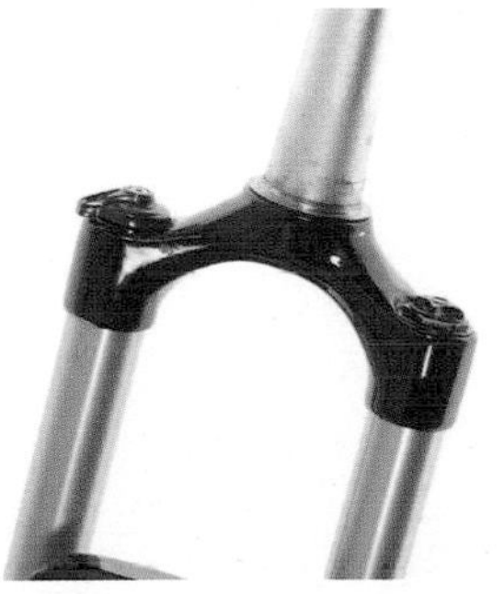

sign of a damaged air seal, while coil forks can break springs and make a scratching sound. Both of these will affect the fork's performance too. Knocking sounds can be caused by worn bushings between the fork stanchion and slider, although they could also be from the headset.

REAR SUSPENSION

The same noises that afflict forks can be made by rear shocks, too. A common issue is clicking or knocking caused by worn shock bushings. Rear suspension pivots can all work loose or wear out too.

BRAKES

The most common brake noise is the dreaded squeal. Many disc brakes squeal under certain conditions, but if they squeal all the time check for contaminated or glazed pads, or loose bolts on the caliper or rotor. Very worn disc pads will whirr, and if you get down to the metal they'll screech. Whirring could also mean a bent or broken pad return spring interfering with the rotor. General rubbing or dragging sounds are usually the result of a misaligned caliper, warped rotor or simply the wheel not being in quite straight.

WHEELS

Loose spokes can make plinking or clicking sounds as they move against one another at the crossing point. Disc brakes put different loads on wheels to rim brakes, and often braking will highlight loose lacing. Retensioning should fix the issue.

A wide range of gears is one of the defining characteristics of the mountain bike. The number of sprockets on the rear wheel has been going relentlessly upward over the years. The original klunkers had just one, then five or six when derailleurs were grafted on. The mid-1980s saw the arrival of indexed gears, with one lever click giving one gear. Seven speeds at the rear became the standard, then eight, nine and now ten (with eleven starting to appear). Front shifting is indexed too, although the traditional triple chainring is being supplanted by double or even single setups.

REAR DERAILLEUR

Indexed gears work by the shifter pulling just the right amount of cable per click to move the derailleur across one sprocket. It's a surprisingly reliable system considering the conditions that it has to work under, but you'll occasionally have to make small adjustments to the cable tension as the cable stretches. You'll have to set the tension correctly if you replace the cable, too. Derailleurs also have adjustable end stops to prevent them shifting the chain off the cassette, and these will need setting up if you've installed a new derailleur.

ADJUSTMENT

1 Different derailleurs have the limit screws in different positions, but they'll all have two located close to one another and labeled H (for High) and L (for Low). Shift into the highest gear (smallest sprocket) and make sure that the H screw prevents the chain from moving any further. If the chain comes off the small sprocket it can get jammed in the gap between sprocket and dropout.

2 Similarly, adjust the limit screw marked L when the gear is in the largest sprocket (lowest gear). Don't worry too much about the indexing working too well at this point, as you need to set the range of the derailleur before tweaking the gears. Double check that the chain can reach this sprocket, but also that the chain cannot jump over the top of the cassette and into the wheel. Also check that the derailleur cannot hit the spokes of the wheel. This can have disastrous consequences, so it is essential that you make sure this cannot happen.

3 With the limit screws correctly set, move on to the indexing. Hold the back wheel off the ground in a workstand, leaving your hands free to pedal the bike and adjust the cable tension. Tension is

adjusted using either the barrel adjuster on the derailleur itself, where the cable enters the body, or – if you have one of the many current derailleurs that don't have a barrel adjuster – the one on the shifter.

4 Start by running through each gear and listening for any noise as you change up the gears, going from the smallest cog to the largest. If it struggles to make the next largest sprocket then the cable is too loose, so you will need to tighten the cable by turning the barrel adjuster counter-clockwise. Now shift across the cassette from large to small sprocket. If there's a delay in the shift or if the chain stays stuck in one gear then the cable is too tight and you will need to loosen it by turning the adjuster clockwise.

5 You should be able to adjust the cable such that shifts are clean and immediate in both directions. If the shift is still bad it may be due to a bent gear hanger, too long (or short) chain, old, dirty, kinked or frayed cables, or worn chain or sprockets.

6 The final check is the angle adjustment screw. This controls how far below the sprockets the upper jockey wheel sits, and needs to be set for different cassettes. Shift into the largest sprocket at the back and small chainring at the front. Adjust the screw so that the upper jockey wheel is just below the sprocket. Turn the screw clockwise to increase the clearance, counter-clockwise to reduce it.

INSTALLATION

1 Check that the hanger is straight and that the threads are clean and uncrossed. The rear gear has to hang perfectly straight. If the hanger is bent or the derailleur cage is twisted, the system will not work. Most aluminum and carbon fiber frames have replaceable hangers. If you have a steel frame with a bent hanger it'll need to be straightened.

2 The chain has to be threaded through the jockey wheels. If there's a chain already installed (perhaps because you're replacing a worn or damaged derailleur), refer to page 42 for splitting and rejoining. If you have a Shimano chain, or a SRAM 10-speed one, it may be easier to remove the bottom jockey wheel from the derailleur to avoid disturbing the chain.

3 Make sure the shifter is in the small sprocket position. Feed the gear cable inner wire into the hole in the derailleur and clamp it under the washer and bolt on the derailleur body. To see how this works, look for a channel molded onto the body of the derailleur. If the cable is clamped to the wrong side of the bolt, shifting will suffer.

4 Screw the gear barrel adjuster fully in, so that there will be plenty of adjustment available when setting the cable. If all the cable outer sections are properly inserted and the gear shifter is in the highest gear position, it should be possible to pull the cable tight enough with your hand. Lock it off with the clamp bolt.

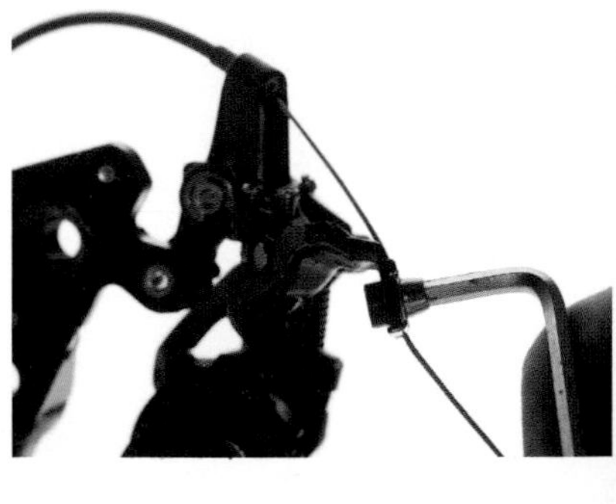

FRONT DERAILLEUR

Front shifting is in some ways more forgiving than rear. The more powerful spring in a front derailleur means that it's better able to deal with a little bit of cable drag, and with a maximum of three chainrings to accommodate, indexing is less critical. Twin-ring setups are even easier. The main challenge is alignment. Direct-mount front derailleurs that attach to a specific tab on the frame are becoming more popular and guarantee good alignment, but the traditional derailleur that clamps around the seat tube needs a little more attention for optimum performance.

ADJUSTMENT

1 Angle the derailleur so that it is exactly parallel with the chainrings. When you buy a new front derailleur it should have a small plastic spacer inside the mechanism. This allows you to align the outside plate of the derailleur cage with the outer (biggest) chainring and position the derailleur over the middle chainring.

2 If the angle is slightly off (as shown here), the shifting will be sloppy. Spend time getting this bit right as it will have the biggest influence on the performance of the derailleur. If it is angled too far outward it will strike the crank when the pedals are turned, making a clonk with each pedal revolution.

3 The vertical distance between the outside derailleur plate and the teeth of the chainring should be no more than 2–3mm. This will ensure that the derailleur is correctly positioned to cope with the difference in size of the granny (smallest) ring and big ring. It also allows for the chain pick-up and will happily clear the teeth of the chainrings.

4 A good chainline is imperative; make sure that the chain can access all of the rear sprockets when in the middle chainring. You can also see that the derailleur in this position is exactly in line with the outer (big) chainring. With the cage correctly aligned, you can remove the spacer from the derailleur.

5 Adjust the limit screw marked L first. Place the rear derailleur in the biggest sprocket, as this is the furthest the chain will travel. Then set the front derailleur so that the chain only just clears the inside of the cage plate. In the granny ring you will probably only use three or four of the lowest gears, so make sure that these are working properly.

6 Next, attach the gear cable. Make sure that the gear shifter is in its lowest position so the cable is at its slackest, and set the barrel adjuster on the shifter a turn out from fully in to give you room for adjustment. In this position the front derailleur will be over the granny ring. Pull the cable through the clamp firmly. Trap the cable in the clamp and check that it's in the right place, as this can affect the shift. Once the cable is pulled through and set you can adjust the low-limit stop screw.

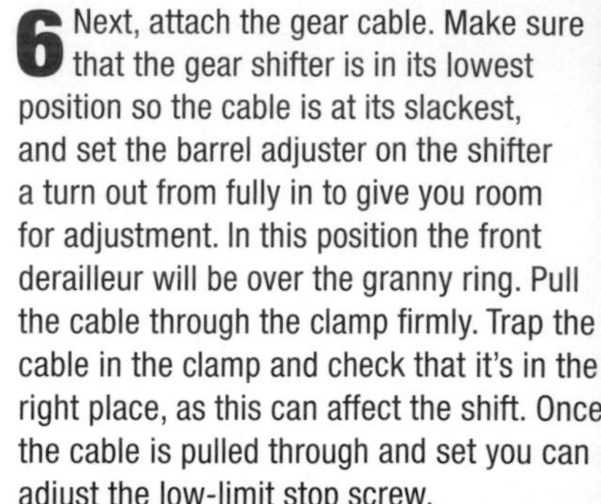

7 Check that the chain shifts cleanly between the inner and middle. If it doesn't want to shift to a larger ring, tighten the cable slightly by turning the barrel adjuster counter-clockwise. If it's hesitant to drop back to a smaller ring, loosen the cable. Check the middle ring to big ring

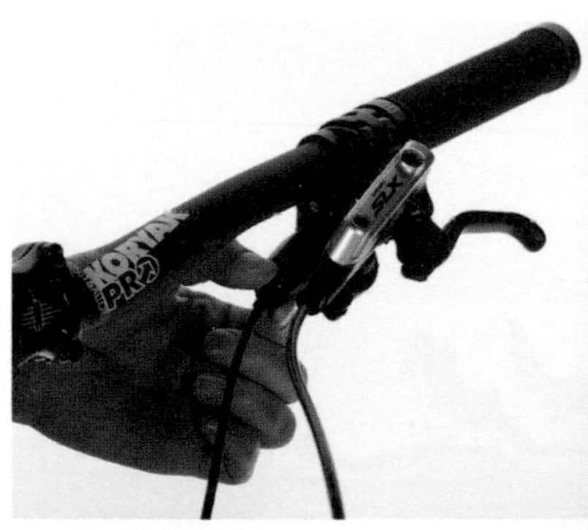

shift in the same way. It shouldn't need further adjustment – if you can't get into the big ring you may need to adjust the high limit screw.

8 Put the chain onto the big chainring and work the rear derailleur through all the gears. You will notice that the chain changes angle considerably, but it will cope with most of the gears on this chainring. Set the limit screw so that in the smallest rear sprocket it just clears the chain.

9 On some full suspension bikes this adjustment can be very tricky. Here the rear swingarm is in the way of the adjustment screws, so you would need to use a longer screwdriver.

INSTALLATION

1 Having obtained the correct replacement derailleur, you'll first need to remove the old one. Most front derailleurs have a screw holding the back of the cage together – removing this allows you to get the chain out of the cage, saving you from splitting the chain. If the front derailleur is riveted together then you'll have to break and rejoin the chain – see page 40-43.

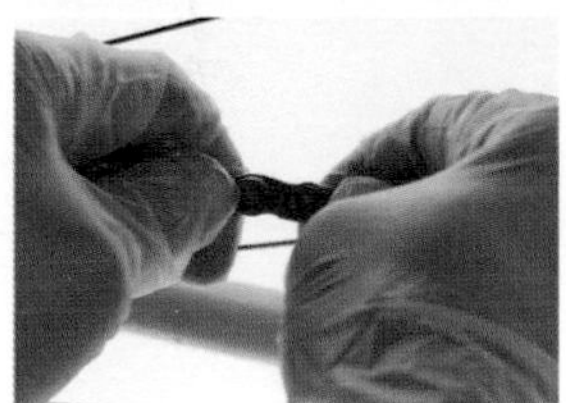

2 With the chain free, loosen the cable pinch bolt and release the cable. Then undo the mounting clamp and remove the old derailleur. You're likely to be able to see clearly where the old derailleur was from marks on the paint. This is a good starting point for positioning the new derailleur. Bolt it on, thread the chain through the cage (either by splitting the chain or removing the cage screw) and see 'Adjustment' instructions.

DERAILLEUR CABLES

Replacing the cables regularly will make your bike shift better and protect the levers from extra wear and tear. The gear cable housing has to be in top condition for the index system to work properly, so always check the cables after crashes as they are very brittle and vulnerable to cracking.

The secret to good cabling is a very good quality, sharp set of cable cutters. Only use your cable cutters for cables, not for spokes and small bolts! Derailleur cables are thin (1.2mm) and flexible, with a small nipple on one end. Don't confuse them with thicker brake cables. Poor shifting can often be fixed simply by replacing the inner wires, and it's worth trying that before replacing the housings as well – inner wires are very cheap.

REPLACING INNER CABLES

1 Inner cables have to be threaded into the shifter first, then routed to the derailleur. The nipple on the end of the cable is pulled by the shifter mechanism in one direction, while the spring in the derailleur pulls the cable back the other way when released. Shimano RapidFire shifters have a cross-headed plug covering the cable access hole.

2 Put the shifter into the highest gear position by clicking the release lever (the smaller, upper lever) repeatedly. With the cable plug removed, the internals of the shifter should now line up so that the cable can be fed through the access hole, emerging at the barrel adjuster. Feed it through all the housing and replace the cable cover.

3 Some SRAM trigger shifters also have a cable port, but many require you to remove the shifter cover. This is secured by either one central bolt, or three at the edges. Some current SRAM units can be detached from the bar clamps and this can make access easier.

4 With the cover off and the shifter clicked to the highest gear, the cable routing will be obvious. Remove the old cable and feed the new one in through the mechanism and out through the barrel adjuster. As with Shimano shifters, feed the cable all the way through the housing and replace the shifter cover.

5 The third common style of shifter is the grip shift. SRAM made its name with grip shifters, although Shimano has some budget units that are found on entry-level MTBs and hybrids. The principle is the same as for other types of shifter – click into the highest gear position, remove the cable access cover, pull out the old cable, push in the new.

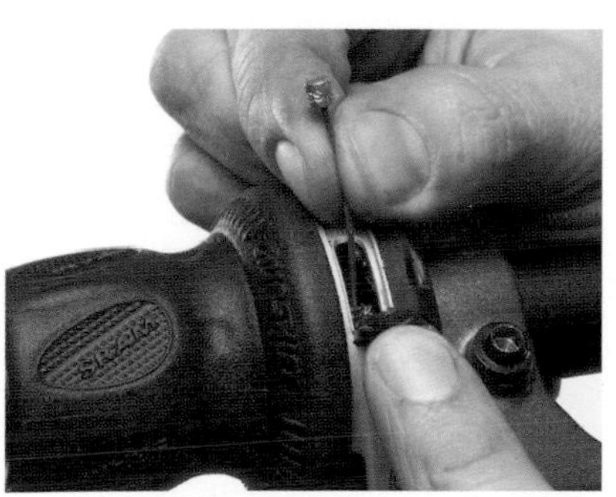

6 Check all the lengths of housing as you thread the inner cable. Cracked or split housing, or missing or damaged ferrules can all hinder shifting. It's also worth installing small O-rings to exposed cable runs to avoid them clattering on the tubes.

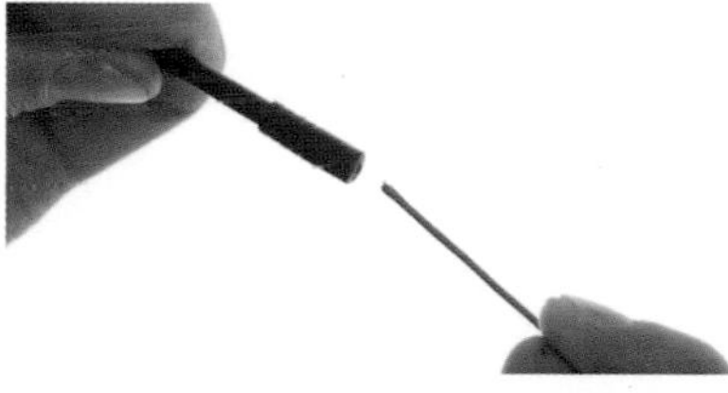

7 Route the cable to the appropriate derailleur (don't get them mixed up – the shifter on the right of the bars is for the rear derailleur), feed it through the cable stop and secure with the clamp bolt. Adjust the shifting as described in this chapter.

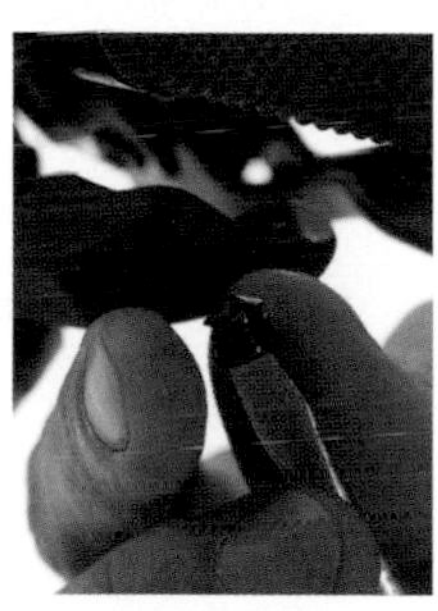

8 Once you're happy with the shifting, give an exposed bit of cable a good yank to make sure all the housings are fully seated in the stops and to get the first bit of cable stretch out of the way. Re-adjust the shifting as appropriate. Cut off any excess cable and crimp on an end cap to prevent fraying.

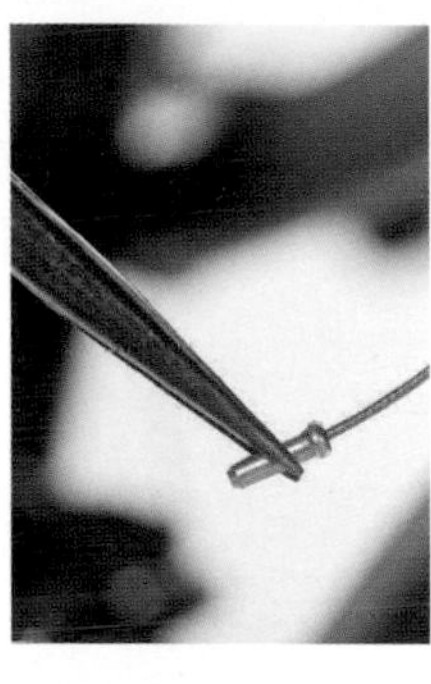

REPLACING CABLE HOUSING

1 Proper cable cutting is the first step in making your gears work properly. Gear cables have a very brittle plastic outer casing, which can be damaged or cracked by using the wrong cutters when cutting them to length. Use cable shears that slice through the cable rather than pliers or cutters that just crush the casing.

2 The derailleur cable housing (below, left) is different from the brake cable housing in that it is made up of strands that travel the length of the housing, inside which is a nylon liner that the derailleur cable can run through. These strands are very hard and cannot be compressed, so they transfer all the effort from the gear shift into bracing the inner cable (or wire). This pulls on the derailleur and in turn pushes the chain onto the next sprocket or chainring.

3 Cutting the housing crimps the cable liners, closing up the hole that the inner wire has to go through. Use an awl or similar tool to make the hole in the liner big enough for the cable to pass through unhindered. This reduces the friction on the cable and enables you to run the inner wires through easily once the cable ferrules are in place.

4 Outer cable ferrules must be applied to the end of each section of cable housing. Cable housing without ferrules will fray and crack at the ends and the cracks will travel up the housing, which doesn't do much for your gear shift and allows water to get into the housing. Eventually, the housing will push its way through the cable guides and the whole system will pack up. Plastic ferrules don't rust and are less likely to seize into the cable guides.

5 Sections of cable housing should change direction as smoothly as possible. Any tight angles will apply pressure to the cable and therefore add friction. This slows the shift and can cause the gears to jump. On suspension bikes it is especially important to make sure that these sections of housing are unhindered and have enough space to move as the bike moves. Check that the bars can turn freely without being hindered by cables.

6 Apply a small smear of grease to the ferrule before you push it into the cable stop or guide. This will make it easier to adjust the cable at the derailleur and also prevent it from getting stuck or seized up.

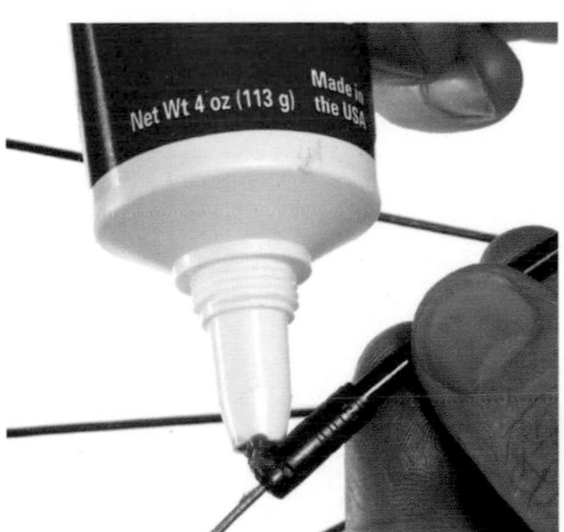

7 There is a seal on the final run of cable housing to the rear derailleur. This is designed to prevent water from running down the cable and into this very sensitive area. Unprotected sections will allow water in and eventually rust the cable and dry the housing so that the whole thing seizes up.

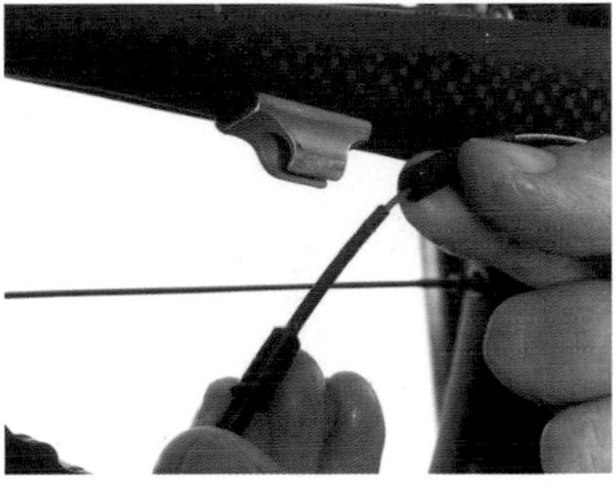

8 Slotted cable guides enable the cable and housing to be completely separated from the bike. This makes lubrication and inspection of the cable easy. To release the cable, place the derailleur in the lowest gear (on the largest sprocket at the back). Then stop pedaling and release the shift lever completely. This will send the cable completely slack, allowing you to release the housing from the guides. ▶

9 On traditional derailleurs with the cable entering from the rear, the final run of housing needs to be long enough to allow the rear derailleur to travel across all the gears – the body of the derailleurs swings as it shifts, and there needs to be enough cable housing to accommodate this without having a huge loop of housing.

10 Shimano Shadow and SRAM derailleurs route the cable from the front, negating the need for the near-180° loop that traditional derailleurs use. They do need a precise length of housing between the last stop on the frame and the stop on the derailleur.

11 Many bikes now use continuous runs of housing all the way from the shifter to the rear derailleur, rather than short lengths between stops and exposed runs along straight sections. This is partly to keep dirt out and partly because a lot of bikes have very few straight tubes.

12 Remember to protect the frame and the paint from the cable housing as vibrations from the trail will cause the housing to wear away at the frame. Place frame stickers where the cables rub, particularly by the handlebars but also at any point where cable housing touches the frame. These sticky protectors will protect the housing from wearing through too.

Even strong riders don't generate much power compared to engines, so it's vital that the bicycle transmission is as efficient as possible. Lab tests have shown bike chains to be 98-99% efficient under ideal conditions, but a mountain bike transmission rarely operates under ideal conditions. It's exposed to the elements, with mud, grit and water all conspiring against it. As a result, it's vital to take good care of the transmission. Regular cleaning and checking for wear is a must. All parts of the transmission – chain, chainrings, sprockets and bottom bracket – should be considered disposable, though, and will need regular replacement.

CHAINS

As the chain wears the distance between the links gets longer. This is commonly referred to as stretch, although it's not really stretching – the pivots and bushings at each link are getting thinner, allowing the pins to move further apart. The cassette sprockets wear as the chain does, eventually reaching the point where a new chain will skip on the old sprockets or chainrings. To avoid having to replace the entire drivetrain, replace chains often. Using a cheap chain and replacing it often – rather than buying an expensive chain and waiting until it wears out the sprockets and chainring too – will turn out cheaper in the long run.

REGULAR CHECKS

1 Measure across 12 full links of the chain (24 pins) with a steel rule. A new chain will measure 12 inches (chains are made in inches, so it's easiest to use inches for this measurement). If it's less than 12 1/16in there's plenty of life in it. Replacing a chain at 12 1/16in usually means that the sprockets and chainrings will be fine with the new chain. If it gets as far as 12 1/8in the sprockets will be quite worn and may skip. Beyond 12 1/8in, skipping with a new chain is almost inevitable.

2 Chain-measuring devices, like the Park one pictured here, are simple to use although less accurate than a ruler. Simply hook one end into the link and use either side to ascertain how much stretch there is in the links. In this case, the gauge will not slot into the corresponding link as the chain is brand new. A worn chain would allow the peg to drop between two rollers. The numbers refer to percent elongation – 1.0% is 1/8in across 12 full links. The 1/16in "safe" point is 0.5%, so if you reach 0.75% on the Park checker it's time to replace the chain.

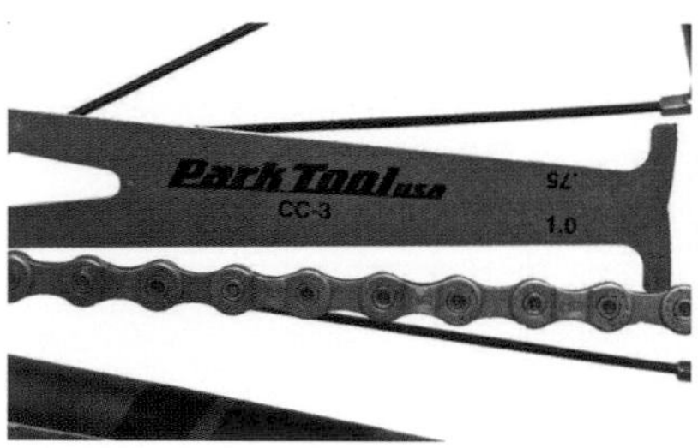

3 You can also assess the state of the chain and the chainrings with a quick visual check. Put the chain on the biggest chainring and smallest cassette sprocket. If you can pull the chain off the chainring and it can clear the tip of one of the chainring teeth, there is some chain wear and it should be replaced.

4 Chain length is critical. Too short and you won't be able to reach all the gears. Too long and shifting will be poor and jumping is likely. The rear derailleur cage should be exactly vertical when the gear is placed in the highest combination (big chainring and small sprocket). If you are replacing a chain, check that this is the case before you remove the old chain.

5 This is the biggest spread of sprocket to chainring that is possible, with the chain pulling the rear derailleur at a very extreme angle. Some mechanics use this position to measure the chain, placing the new chain around this chainring/sprocket combination and adding two links to allow for the derailleur. Some full suspension systems move the rear axle further away from the bottom bracket as they compress – do this check with the rear shock deflated or unbolted at one end to allow for this.

6 Ideally the derailleur also needs to be able to take up all the slack chain in the small chainring/small sprocket combination. With a triple crankset and a very wide gear range this may not be possible, although you'll only be using the three or four largest sprockets when in the inner chainring.

REMOVING AND JOINING SHIMANO CHAINS

Originally chains could be split or rejoined simply by pushing one rivet out with a chain tool and then pushing it back in again. The demands of multiple gears and narrow chains means that this is no longer possible. Shimano chains use a special non-reusable joining pin. Make sure you get the correct chain for your bike. They're different widths for different numbers of gears, and must match – a 10-speed transmission needs a 10-speed chain.

1 This flat-ended pin marks the spot where the chain was first joined. You can break the chain anywhere except at this pin. Remove the old chain and, assuming that it was the correct length, measure the new one next to it. You'll usually have to remove a few links from one end. Thread the new chain through the rear derailleur jockey wheels, front derailleur cage and over the chainrings. Rest it on the bottom bracket for now.

2 Leaving the chain off the chainrings will give you some slack and make it easier to re-join the two ends. The special Shimano joining pin has a narrow, pointed part to make sure that the link is pushed in the correct way. You need a pin that's the right width for the chain you're joining – 10-speed ones are narrower than nine.

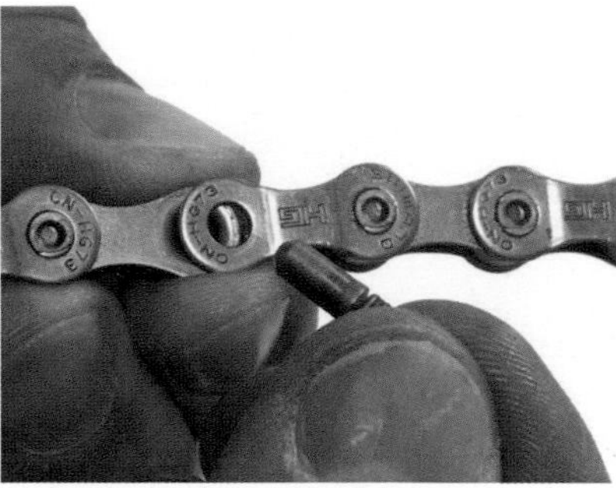

3 Push the link through using a quality Shimano-compatible chain-tool. This Park tool has shaped jaws to prevent the side plates becoming squeezed together. Keep the chain straight and turn the handle firmly and slowly to make sure that the pin goes through straight.

4 You need to push the pin right through so that the pointed end comes out of the other side of the chain. You'll feel a slight click as the pin reaches the right point. Back off the handle of the chain tool and check that the fatter part of the pin is equally spaced on either side of the link plates.

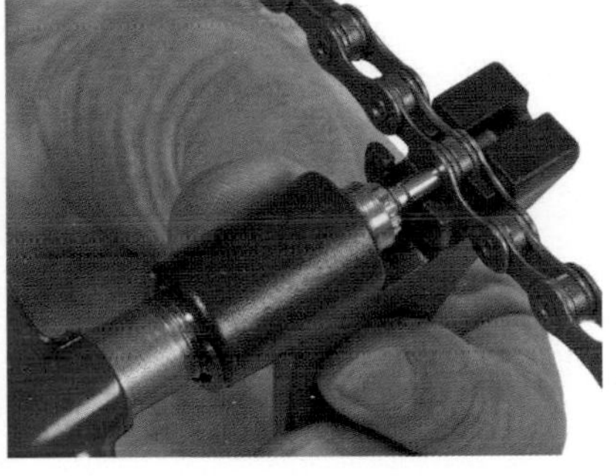

5 Once you're happy that the pin is in the right place, snap off the pointed end by gripping it with pliers and twisting it off. It will snap cleanly off. With the guide pin broken off, you can run the bike through the gears and make sure everything is working.

6 If the chain jumps, the freshly joined link may be slightly stiff. To remove a stiff link, first add some lube to it and push it into an inverted V shape. Then place your thumbs on the links adjacent to this link. Grip the chain and gently push the chain against itself. This very careful 'bending' should free the link immediately.

SRAM CHAINS

Rather than a special joining pin, SRAM chains use a joining link. Eight and 9-speed links are called Power Links and are reusable. Ten-speed links are called Power Locks and can only be used once – they need a chain tool to remove. You'll need to shorten the chain to the right length in the usual way but ensure that you remove the side plates – the Power Link/Lock joins the chain between two rollers. Joining a Power Link involves pushing one link pin through each roller, pushing the two plates together so the pins go through the holes and then pulling the ends of the chain apart so it clicks shut.

CASSETTE SPROCKETS

All but the very cheapest bikes have the freewheel mechanism integrated into the rear hub (known as a freehub), with the sprockets in a cassette that slides on to the hub and is secured by a lockring. Even if the cassette doesn't need replacing, it's worth removing periodically to clean behind it. You'll need to remove it to service the hub, too.

When replacing cassettes, make sure you get the appropriate part. The Shimano-pattern freehub has become an industry standard, so 8, 9 and 10-speed cassettes and hubs from all manufacturers are generally interchangeable. Seven-speed cassettes use the same spline pattern but the freehub is narrower, so cassettes with more sprockets won't fit (and you'll need a spacer to fit a 7-speed cassette onto an 8-speed freehub). SRAM's 11-speed system uses a different freehub body. You need to get a cassette with the same number of sprockets as the one you're replacing, unless you're upgrading, in which case you'll need new shifters too (and possibly other parts).

1 Remove the cassette using a chain whip and a cassette-removing tool. The chain whip prevents the cassette from turning, and should be positioned so that the chain on the tool can wrap around the sprocket enough to prevent it from spinning when you push on the wrench.

2 The lock ring threads into the cassette body and secures the sprockets. Because the cassette is integral to the drive, it needs to be tight. The serrated teeth pressed into the last sprocket and the underside of the lock ring prevent it from vibrating loose.

3 The first two or three cassette sprockets will be loose, so be careful not to drop them. Lay the wheel flat on the work-bench and take the sprockets off one by one, placing them down in the order in which they came off the wheel.

4 Once the loose cassette sprockets and washers have been removed, the main cassette cluster can slide off. There is a series of slots cut into the cassette body. These are shaped so that the sprockets can only be returned the right way around.

5 Apply a thin layer of grease or anti-seize to the cassette body before you slide the cassette back into place. This will prevent the cassette body from rusting as water can get into the cassette very easily. If there is any corrosion on the body, use a fine wire brush to clean it off. A brass suede shoe brush is good to have in your tool kit for this type of job.

6 Lastly, replace the cassette cluster, the washers, the loose sprockets and the lock ring. Then tighten the lock ring to 35–50Nm. You'll be surprised how tight this is, but the cassette bears a considerable load and needs to be checked for tightness regularly. If you don't have a torque wrench, it's a decent push with a 12in wrench – you should hear a number of clicks from the lockring.

CRANKS, CHAINRINGS AND BOTTOM BRACKETS

REMOVING AND REPLACING CRANKS

OUTBOARD BEARING, PRESSFIT AND BB30

1 Removing modern two-piece cranks is very straightforward, but there are a few variations in how they work. Shimano cranksets have the axle permanently fixed to the drive-side crank arm. To remove the left-hand arm, first loosen the two opposing Allen bolts.

2 With the bolts loosened, you'll be able to undo the plastic preload cap using the Shimano TL-FC16 tool (other tool companies make compatible tools, but the simple plastic Shimano one is all you need). Some Shimano cranks have a stopper plate in the clamp slot – flick this upward to disengage its pin from the hole in the axle.

3 The left-hand crank should now pull off by hand. It may take a bit of waggling to loosen it from the splines on the axle. If it really won't move, make sure the bolts are loose and that the stopper plate is disengaged. If everything is loose, a gentle tap to the back of the arm with a rubber mallet should pop it off.

4 With the left-hand crank removed, the right-hand crank and axle can be pulled out. Some Shimano cranksets have O-ring seals on the axle next to the bottom bracket bearings – be careful not to lose these. The axle may need a gentle tap on the exposed end with a rubber mallet to free it from the bearings.

5 SRAM cranksets come in two versions. GXP models are very similar to Shimano, with the axle permanently attached to the drive-side crank and the left-hand crank fitting onto splines on the end of the axle. The main difference is that the left-hand crank is secured by a bolt that threads into the end of the axle, like an old-style bottom bracket. The bolt is held behind a cap so that undoing the bolt with an 8mm Allen wrench pushes the arm off the axle. With the arm removed, the axle and drive-side crank pull out in the same way as Shimano units.

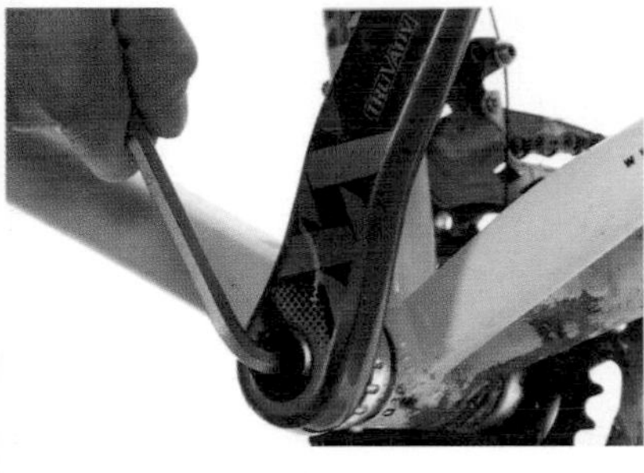

6 SRAM cranksets with 30mm axles for BB30 and Pressfit 30 bottom brackets work the other way around, with a 10mm Allen bolt on the drive-side that pushes the right-hand crankarm and chainrings off the axle. Depending on the exact setup, there'll be various spacers and shims on the axle – take careful note of the order these are in so you can put them back correctly.

7 Be sure that you attempt to undo the correct crankarm on a SRAM chainset. The non-removable arm may have a tempting-looking bolt head, but this should not be undone. If you're not sure, take a close look – the non-removable bolt should have 'Do not remove' engraved on it.

8 In all cases, re-installation is the reverse of removal. Make sure that all the spacers are in place on the axle, and use a rubber mallet to seat the side of the crankset that carries the axle into the bearings – use tape to protect the face of the crankarm. Place the removable crank arm onto the splines. SRAM cranks need tightening to 48-54Nm, which is substantial; 30mm units have a preload adjuster behind the crank which needs adjusting until it contacts the bearing face. For Shimano cranks, tighten the preload cap finger tight, then tighten the pinch bolts alternately to 10-15Nm.

SQUARE TAPER, ISIS AND OCTALINK

1 The traditional bottom bracket setup has the axle and bearings as one unit, with a crankarm fitting on each end (rather than the axle being permanently attached to one or the other and the bottom bracket just being the bearings). Usually the fixing bolt has an 8mm Allen head with the washer as an integral part of the bolt and an integrated plastic dust cap. Older cranks will use a 14 or 15mm hex-headed bolt and washer protected by a separate dust cap.

2 Unlike two-piece cranksets, traditional units won't just pull off by hand (unless they're broken). You need a crank puller to pull them off the bottom bracket axle. The puller screws into the extractor threads that will be revealed once you've removed the bolts and washer. Clean out any mud from the crank threads with a squirt of spray lube. Undo the center bolt of the puller, then thread the outer part into the crank. Make sure it goes in straight. ISIS and Octalink cranks require a larger head on the crank pulling tool – a puller designed for a square taper axle will just go inside the larger splined axles.

3 Once you have correctly inserted the puller, tighten the plunger. The tool shown has an integrated handle, some pullers have a hex head that you'll need to turn with a wrench. The arm rests on the end of the axle and the pushing/pulling motion forces the crank off the square axle taper. Make sure the outside part of the puller is fully inserted. If you strip the extractor threads in the crank you'll need to replace it.

4 Keep hold of the crank otherwise it'll fall on the floor when it comes off the axle. Remove the crank puller and repeat the procedure on the opposite crank. With both cranks off you have access to the bottom bracket. This is an ISIS crank – Octalink cranks are similar but the spline pattern is very different. Don't mix them up.

5 To re-install, clean the splines on the ends of the axle and the inside of the crank and apply a smear of grease. ISIS and Octalink cranks have a stop on the axle so the cranks always go on by the same amount. It's still a good idea to use a torque wrench to tighten them correctly.

CHAINLINE

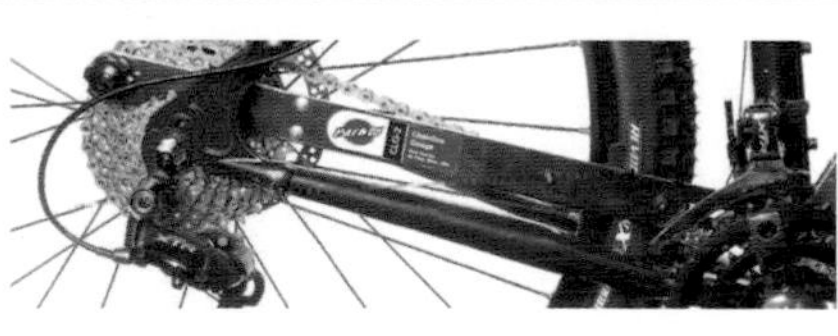

For ideal shifting you really want the chain to be at its straightest in the middle chainring (on a triple) and in the middle of the cassette, allowing for optimum spread of gears with less chain angle. This improves shifting, prolongs the life of the chain and prevents it from coming off unexpectedly. In practice, the chainrings are usually slightly more outboard than this in the interest of frame clearance. Double cranksets should align the center of the cassette (between two sprockets on 8 or 10-speed) with a point halfway between the two rings. This chainline tool lets you check the alignment, although modern bottom bracket systems make it hard to get it wildly wrong.

REMOVING AND REPLACING BOTTOM BRACKETS

With the crankarms out of the way, the bottom bracket itself is accessible. The majority of modern bottom brackets, whichever type they are, are essentially non-serviceable and are simply replaced when worn. Some high-end internal cartridge units have replaceable bearings, though – it's worth checking before replacing the whole thing. It's also possible to replace just the bearings in many outboard bearing units, but while this can save some money it's a bit awkward and not recommended by the manufacturers. Outboard BBs are relatively inexpensive and easy to install anyway.

Whether square taper, ISIS or Octalink, all internal threaded bottom brackets are removed and installed in the same way. The same is true for outboard bearings, although again they're not necessarily cross-compatible with different cranksets (see above right).

OUTBOARD BEARINGS

1 To remove an outboard bearing, use the appropriate C wrench – this is a Shimano one, most tool brands have their own version – to unscrew it. Remember that the right (drive) side has a left-hand thread and unscrews clockwise. The left (non-drive) side has a conventional right-hand thread.

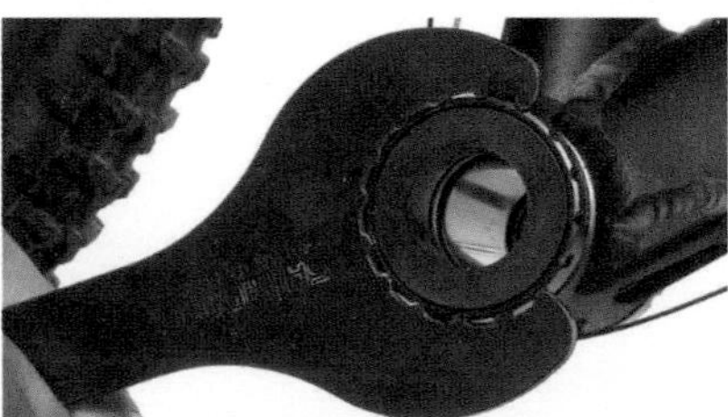

BOTTOM BRACKET COMPATIBILITY

While the various brands of outboard bearing bottom bracket look the same, they're not interchangeable. Shimano and Race Face systems use 24mm axles, but SRAM uses a stepped axle that's 24mm on one side and 25mm on the other, and can only be used with specific bottom brackets. FSA cranks also use 24mm axles, although it's safest to stick with FSA bearings – there are sometimes tolerance issues that mean a poor fit with Shimano (or compatible) units. Aftermarket manufacturers like Hope make bottom brackets for all systems.

2 With the bottom bracket shell empty, make sure that it's faced on both sides. If the faces of the shell aren't parallel and flat, the bearing housings could become distorted or misaligned when fully tightened. You will find that some frames need more preparation than others. Clean out any swarf from the bottom bracket and use some anti-seize grease on the threads.

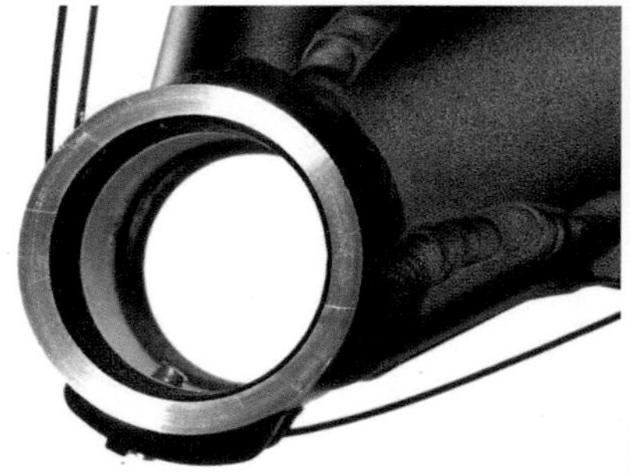

3 Depending on the width of the bottom bracket shell, you'll need spacers for correct spacing and chainline. Measure the width of the bottom bracket shell – it will be either 68mm or 73mm. 68mm shells require two spacers on the right and one on the left. A 73mm shell requires one spacer on the right. If you have a bottom bracket mount front derailleur or chain device, that takes the place of a right-hand spacer – on a 73mm shell there would be no spacers, just the derailleur or chain device plate.

4 Install the internal plastic cover to the right (drive) side cup and thread it into the bottom bracket shell. Remember that the drive side is a left-hand thread (tightens counter-clockwise). Screw it in finger tight – if it won't turn easily, make sure it's not cross-threaded. Repeat for the non-drive side cup. Finally use the C wrench to tighten both cups to 35-50Nm and re-install the crank arms.

BB30 AND PRESSFIT

BB30 and Pressfit bottom brackets, with an oversized, unthreaded bottom bracket shell, need the old bearings to be removed with a special tool and the new one pushed in with special adaptors on a headset press. While it's entirely possible to use improvised tools, the possibility for expensive frame damage means it's a job best left to a shop. If you already have a headset press, though, it's exactly the same procedure as replacing press-in headset cups.

SQUARE TAPER, ISIS AND OCTALINK

1 Most conventional bottom brackets use the same splined tool to remove and install, although ISIS and Octalink units need a tool with a larger hole in the middle to accommodate the bigger axle. Undo the non-drive side first – this is usually a separate removable cup. Turn the tool with a ratchet handle or large wrench, taking care not to let it slip in the splines. Repeat for the drive side. Remember that the drive side unscrews clockwise.

2 Clean out the frame's bottom bracket shell thoroughly with a degreaser and dry it off. Then dress all the threads with plenty of anti-seize or quality synthetic grease. The bottom bracket is often neglected for many months, so how easy it is to remove depends on how well it was prepared before it was put in.

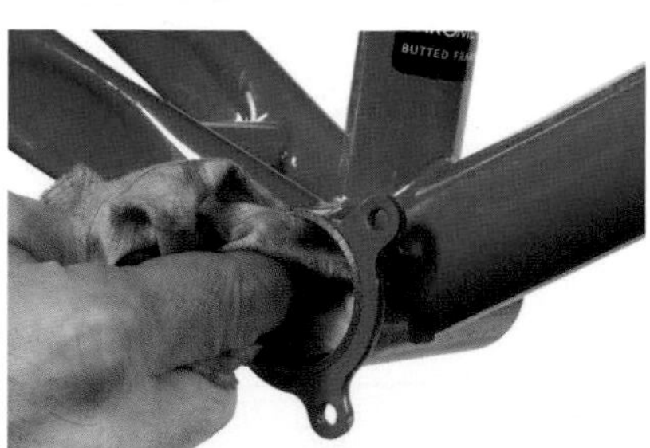

3 The new unit will have one removable side, which is usually on the non-drive side. Pull this off so that the unit can be installed into the drive side first. This side has a left-hand thread and tightens counter-clockwise. If the threads have been properly prepared, you will be able to turn the unit with your fingers. Spin it in until there is about 1cm of thread left. You will now be able to insert the non-drive-side cup. This tightens clockwise and will mesh with the cartridge inside the shell. Most Shimano brackets have a taper on the inside that allows them to self-locate. Again, tighten this with your fingers until there is about 1cm of thread left showing.

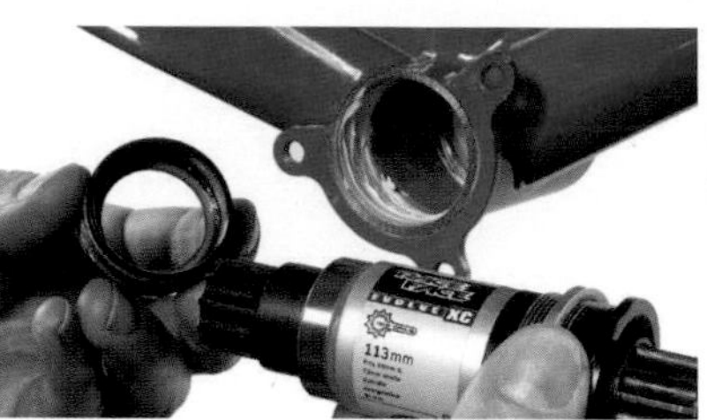

4 Use the bottom bracket tool to tighten the unit into the frame. Make sure that the shoulder of the unit on the drive side is tight up against the frame first. This is to make sure that the chainset will sit in the right place and that it will not loosen. Once the drive side is tight you can tighten the non-drive side. Tighten both cups to 40–50Nm, then install the cranks.

REPLACING CHAINRINGS

1 It's possible to remove and replace chainrings with the crankarms mounted on the bike – they can be wriggled out over the crank spider. However, modern cranksets are so easy to remove that you might as well do so. It makes it a lot easier to get at the inner chainring bolts. Undo these with a 5mm Allen wrench.

2 With the bolts removed, the inner ring can be lifted off. You'll need to take the inner chainring off even if you're only aiming to replace the middle or outer. When mounted, the inner ring blocks access to the sleeve nuts for the bigger rings.

3 The bolts for the outer chainrings undo from the outside. Be very careful not to cut your hand on the outer chainring as the bolts come loose. With a bit of thought you can orient the Allen wrench so that you can squeeze it toward the crank arm.

4 If you're lucky, the sleeve nuts will stay put and you'll be able to unwind the bolts from the other side. If the nuts spin, you'll need to use this special wrench to hold them via the slots in their outer face.

5 With all the bolts and sleeve nuts removed, the two outer chainrings (or one chainring and a bashguard, or just the big ring if it's a double crankset) will come free. Twist the outer chainring so it clears the mounting tabs and lift it off.

6 When replacing the rings, pay attention to the orientation. The ramps and pins must align correctly for optimum shifting. The outermost ring will have a peg on it that should go behind the crank. The others will have a nub on the inner circumference that also aligns with the crank.

7 It can be a little tricky getting the outer two chainrings together. Once you've got one bolt in the rest are easier. Use anti-seize grease on the bolt threads and on the outside of the sleeve nuts. This will make them easier to remove next time. Tighten the bolts in a crosswise fashion, not in a circle.

8 Some cranks have detachable spiders, allowing different ring sizes (or a single ring with integrated spider) to be installed. Different cranks need different tools for the spiders – this one uses a Shimano lock ring tool.

Brakes have come a long way since the Californian "klunker" pioneers. Their earliest bikes used coaster brakes in the rear hub, activated by putting backward pressure on the pedals. The famous Repack descent got its name because the riders had to strip and regrease their coaster hubs each run – the grease would boil out from the heat generated by the brake.

Modern hydraulic disc brakes, as found on nearly all mountain bikes, are much more reliable and powerful. They need a lot less maintenance but still require some looking after for the best performance.

DISC BRAKES

REPLACING DISC BRAKE PADS

Once installed and aligned, hydraulic disc brakes require little maintenance beyond keeping them clean. The most frequent task is replacing the pads. Brake pad lifespan is affected by numerous factors – pad compound, soil type, riding style, weather conditions and more. A set of pads could last for months, or they might be destroyed in a single day. It's a good idea to carry at least one spare pair of pads on rides just in case the latter occurs – they don't take up much room. Hydraulic brakes self-adjust as the pads wear, but only up to a point. If the brake lever starts getting closer to the bar, it's probably time for new ones. Eventually you'll wear through all the friction material and the metal backing plates will contact the rotor. This is both noisy and ineffective. It'll also damage the rotor.

We're using Shimano brakes here, but the principles are the same for most brakes. Note that pads from other brakes aren't interchangeable.

1 Remove the wheel (see page 80-84). Pads are held into calipers by some form of retaining pin. It may be a threaded pin that unscrews, sometimes with a c-clip on one end to stop it coming loose. Or, as here, it may be a simple split pin. Split pins usually have the end bent over to keep them in, so straighten that with pliers first.

2 With the split pin straightened (or c-clip removed) pull out (or unscrew) the pin. It will usually pass through a tab on each brake pad, as well as the pad return spring sandwiched between them.

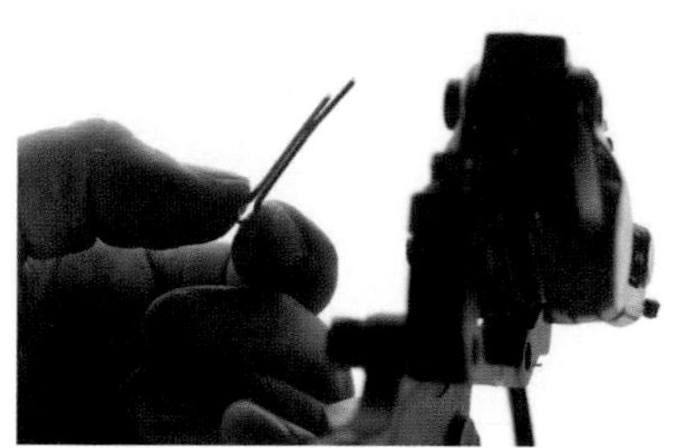

3 Hydraulic brakes self-adjust for pad wear, which means that the pistons will be too close together to fit new pads. To retract them, use a broad, flat-bladed screwdriver to gently lever the old pads apart. The old pads will protect the pistons. Cable-operated discs will need to be adjusted out manually.

4 The pads and spring will simply lift out of the caliper. Squeeze them together and pull. On these Shimano brakes they come out upward – some brakes require the pads to be taken out downward, it's usually obvious which it is.

5 Assemble the new pads and spring. The prongs of the spring should sit on either side of the friction material on the pad, resting on the backing plate. Some brakes have left- and right-handed pads, on others it doesn't matter.

6 Push the new pads and spring into the caliper, making sure they go fully home. Some brakes have internal clips or magnets to hold the pads. Replace the retaining pin – if it won't go in, the pads aren't inserted correctly. Put the wheel back in and pump the brake lever a few times to reset the calipers.

INSTALLING BRAKE ROTORS

Brake rotors don't need replacing very often, but they do wear out eventually. They last a lot longer if you refresh your pads regularly and keep the calipers and rotors clean. You're more likely to have to replace one because it gets bent. Remember that the rotor-to-pad spacing is around 0.5mm so it won't take much of a buckle to mess it up. You'll also need to remove them to service your hubs and it's a good idea to take them off if you're packing your bike into a box to travel so they don't get damaged. There are two mounting standards for MTB brake rotors.

SIX-BOLT ROTORS

1 The most common rotor configuration is the six-bolt type, using six equally spaced bolts to secure the rotor to a flat face on the end of the hub shell. Make sure that the rotor is oriented correctly on the hub. There'll be a rotation arrow marked on the rotor.

2 This Shimano rotor uses anti-rotation washers to help prevent the rotor bolts from working loose. Each washer has two holes and bridges across between two adjacent bolts.

3 Apply Threadlock or a similar product to the bolt threads and tighten the rotor bolts to 4Nm. They usually need a six-sided Torx driver. Tighten each bolt a quarter-turn at a time, moving on to the opposite bolt and working around until they're all tight so as not to distort the rotor.

4 Once the rotor is in place you can "set" the washers by bending them to sit flat with the head of the rotor bolt, which is three-sided. This is an added precaution that prevents the bolts from vibrating loose. Once the disc is installed, leave it for a few hours before you ride to give the Threadlock a chance to set properly.

CENTERLOCK ROTORS

1 Shimano's Centerlock mounting system uses a splined carrier on the end of the hub onto which the special rotor slides. It's a simple system that's easier to use than the six-bolt setup.

2 Apply a little anti-seize grease to the splines, being careful not to get any on the rotor itself. Carefully slide the new rotor onto the hub splines and push it home.

3 Put a little more anti-seize on the threads of the lockring and screw it into the end of the hub. Do it up finger-tight. If it won't tighten, make sure the threads are clean and undamaged.

4 Using a lockring tool (the splines are the same as a cassette lockring), tighten the lockring securely. It's best to use a torque wrench – 40Nm is the number to aim for.

5 Hubs with 20mm through-axles use the same rotor but a different lockring. The standard lockring is too small for a 20mm axle to pass through, so a larger lockring is used.

6 The bigger lockring is tightened using the same C-wrench as you'd use for outboard bottom bracket bearings. Tighten it securely.

INSTALLING AND ALIGNING DISC BRAKE CALIPERS

Installing new disc calipers does take time to get right, although it's become easier. For a long time the ISO mount, with two bolts running sideways, was the standard, relying on tricky shims to get the alignment right. Most brakes now are post mount, with bolts running front and back and slotted holes in the calipers. The calipers will either be mounted directly to the frame and fork, or there'll be an extra adapter between them. This is very common on rear brakes – ISO mounts are still common on frames, with an adapter allowing the use of a post-mount caliper. Different sized adapters are available to accommodate different rotor sizes.

1 Secure the brake caliper to the fork or frame, including the appropriate adapter. If the caliper is post mount, tighten the bolts that hold the adapter to the frame and fork first, alternating between them. Then mount the caliper to the adapter, but don't tighten the bolts fully yet. Add some Threadlock to the bolts.

2 The calipers must be centered over the rotor, rather than over the pads themselves, to make sure that the pads wear evenly and to prevent vibration and any nasty noises. Make sure that the wheel is tight in the frame – if it isn't, it can slightly affect the final rotor and caliper positions.

3 Post-mount brakes are very easy to align. The caliper is mounted on slotted bolt-holes, which allow a fair bit of side-to-side movement. With the bolts slightly loosened and the wheel in the fork or frame, pull the brake lever. The caliper will center itself on the rotor – tighten the bolts to secure, then release the brake.

4 ISO brakes are trickier. Tighten both bolts then check the alignment visually. If it's off to one side, add shims (available in a range of thicknesses down to 0.2mm) between the mount and caliper – the mount is usually a little further out than it needs to be. Retighten the bolts and check again. It usually takes a few iterations to get it right.

5 Once you're happy that the rotor is centered in the caliper, tighten the fixing bolts. As a general guide, the setting will usually be 6Nm, which is not as tight as you'd expect. Take great care not to overtighten them, especially on post-mount frames or forks – stripping the threads in the frame or fork is bad news.

CONTACT POINTS

You and your bike meet at five points – one saddle, two pedals and two handlebar grips. These points between them have to take all your weight and transfer all your pedaling efforts to the transmission. Turns, wheelies, jumps and all other maneuvers are initiated through the contact points, so it's essential that they're all in top condition, secure and reliable.

HANDLEBARS

The trend for mountain bike bars is toward more width. In the early 1990s a 580mm (23in) bar was considered wide, but that would be exceptionally narrow by today's standards. XC race bikes may still be equipped with flat 580mm bars, but for all-round trail bikes even 680mm (26.75in) is on the narrow side – plenty of bikes come with 720mm (28.4in) or wider, and it's possible to get bars over 760mm (30in) wide.

Such wide bars work well with modern bikes, which tend to have relaxed head angles and short stems. Such a setup isn't for everyone, though, especially if you're below average height or ride densely wooded trails. While it's best to buy handlebars at the length you are going to use them, that's not always practical – bars aren't usually available in a large range of widths, with manufacturers assuming that you'll cut them down to suit you. It's possible to cut down aluminum and carbon bars.

1 Before installing handlebars, ensure that the inside of the stem clamp is free from any sharp edges or burrs that may lead to stress risers in the bar and possible failure. Sharp corners at the edge of the bar clamp can be easily rectified with a small half-round needle file.

2 Even with a perfectly smooth bar clamp, take care when installing bars not to twist them in the stem too much. This can scratch the surface of the bar, which creates a stress riser and can fail at a later date. There is usually a mark or series of marks on the bar where the center section is. This will also give you an idea of the preferred angle of the sweep. Line this up with the front cap of the stem.

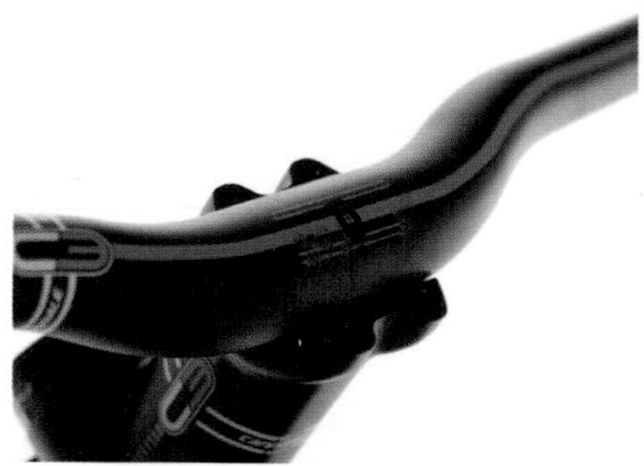

3 Almost every mountain bike stem has a detachable face plate, allowing the bars to be removed without disturbing the shifters, brake levers or grips. It's essential to tighten the faceplate bolts evenly. For the common four-bolt face plate, tighten the bolts a little at a time going from one corner to the opposite corner, then across or up, then diagonally to the final bolt. At this stage tighten them just enough to stop the bar rotating.

4 Center the bars in the stem. Again, there are usually guide marks on the bar to show you where this is. If in doubt, measure from each side of the bar clamp to the ends of the bars. If it needs to move, you may need to slightly loosen the clamp bolts again.

5 Most mountain bikes have riser bars, with the grip sections positioned higher than the center. Angle the bars so that the sweep of the grip sections is up and back, roughly in line with your arms when seated. On most bars this position coincides with the center section of the bar being in a vertical plane.

6 Position the controls at equal distances from the stem. Do not over-tighten them, as the levers are sensitive and could bend if they are not allowed to 'move' a little in the event of a crash. Usually the brake levers and shifters have their own separate clamps.

7 Sometimes the brake lever and shifter will share a clamp – this is SRAM's Matchmaker system. The controls are still independently adjustable, but there's just a single bolt securing them to the bars.

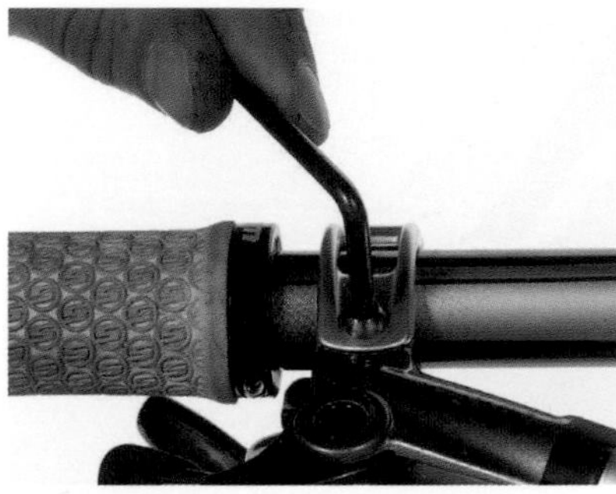

8 Finish off with final tightening of the stem clamp bolts. Then install the grips. Check the angle of the bar and positions of the controls, and check all the bolts for tightness before riding.

HANDLEBAR TIPS

1. Most creaking noises from handlebars can easily be eliminated by stripping the bar from the stem, cleaning it with parts cleaner (disc-brake cleaner is good for this) and rebuilding the stem with fresh grease or copper slip on the fixing bolts. Take the stem off, check the steerer for corrosion and clean it too. Take the opportunity to inspect the bars – if there are any cracks, deep gouges or mysterious discoloration, replace them.

2. Bars don't last forever. They can be damaged in crashes, and in the case of carbon fiber bars damage isn't always visible. Aluminum bars will eventually fatigue and start to crack, although this could take many years. Several manufacturers recommend replacing bars and stems every two to three years even if they haven't been crashed. The consequences of a sudden bar or stem failure are unlikely to be pleasant, so regular replacement is a good idea.

SADDLE AND SEATPOST

1 The seatpost should be greased regularly (unless it's made out of carbon fiber, for which a specific carbon-friendly assembly paste should be used). It's likely that you'll want to lower the seatpost out on the trail for long rocky descents and technical sections, which means you'll need to be able to move the saddle quickly. A seatpost can seize up very fast if you neglect to regrease it regularly.

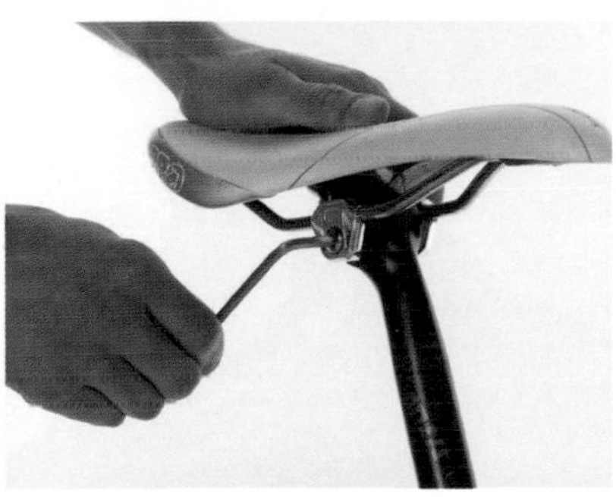

2 The seatpost is held into the frame with a clamp, either with a quick-release lever or a simple bolt. To change the saddle height, simply undo the lever (or bolt), move the post to the appropriate height and retighten. If the seatpost slips, tighten the clamp more, but don't overdo it. If you're having to really heave on it, grease the cam section of the quick-release lever. If it's a clamp with a bolt, grease the threads and under the head of the bolt.

3 To adjust the fore and aft position of the saddle, loosen the clamp at the top of the seatpost that holds the saddle rails. This will vary depending on the style of seatpost – some have two bolts. With the clamp loosened, slide the saddle to your desired position and retighten.

4 The saddle should be level across the top – line it up with a brick wall or use a level to check this. If you have a single-bolt seatpost you'll be able to tilt the saddle with the bolt loosened as for the fore and aft adjustment. Some seatposts have two bolts, one in front of the post and one behind. Loosening the rear bolt and tightening the front will drop the nose of the saddle and vice versa.

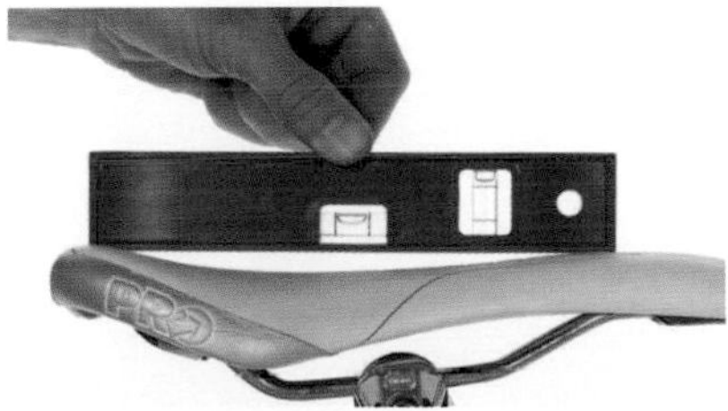

FINDING THE RIGHT RIDING POSITION

There's a degree of subjectivity and personal preference to some aspects of riding position, but until you've worked out what your preferences are aim for a simple, balanced position. Get a friend to help you, take photographs or use a full length mirror to help you get the best balanced position.

SADDLE HEIGHT

Saddle height is one of the most important adjustments on any bike. It's slightly less critical on a mountain bike than on a road bike because of the different ways bikes are ridden. On a road bike you spend a lot of time seated and pedaling, on a mountain bike you're constantly moving between standing and sitting, pedaling and coasting.

The best rule of thumb for saddle height is that the knee should be slightly bent at the bottom of the pedal stroke. An easy way to judge this is to adjust the saddle height so that your leg is fully extended with your heel on the pedal (while wearing the shoes you'll be riding in) at the bottom of the pedal stroke, with the crank arm in line with the seat tube (see above). This should mean that when you put the ball of your foot on the pedal you have the appropriate slightly bent leg.

TOO LOW

With the saddle at the right height your upper legs will end up slightly below horizontal at the top of the pedal stroke. If your legs come up higher than that, your

seat is too low for efficient pedaling and will put excessive strain on the knees. A very low saddle is great for steep, tricky descents but don't ride for prolonged periods like this.

Some riders choose to set their saddles very slightly (up to an inch) lower than the optimum pedaling height for a bit more clearance off-road, and if your riding involves a lot of out-of-the-saddle work that can be a useful compromise.

TOO HIGH

This often creates back problems as the rider will have to stretch to reach the pedals at the bottom of each stroke, which tilts the pelvis and pulls on the lower back muscles. The same principle applies if you bob back and forth excessively when riding hard as your back will tire and start to hurt. This is often why back pain is especially bad after a hard hilly ride or race.

SADDLE FORE/AFT POSITION

The traditional rule of thumb for front and back saddle position is that the center of your knee should be vertically above the pedal spindle when sitting on the bike with pedals level. Don't be too worried about getting this exactly right – it's a good starting point, but different riders have different preferences. Equally important on a mountain bike is the reach to the bars, which affects weight distribution and control. Don't be afraid to set your saddle slightly further forward or backward from the standard position for comfort or control.

STEM AND BAR POSITION

The other key ingredients of bike fit are the stem and bars. The trend for most mountain bikes is for shorter stems (90mm or shorter) and wider bars (680-720mm is common), which give more control and a slightly more upright riding position. Even cross-country race bikes are going this way.

Usually your bike will have come with a bar and stem appropriate for the size of bike and intended use, but since one bike size covers quite a range of rider sizes you may need to change one or the other. Swapping the stem for one slightly shorter or longer can make a useful difference if you're at one end or other of the range, but be wary of changing to a stem more than 10-15mm different from the original. You're aiming for a balanced position, with weight evenly distributed between bars and saddle when seated.

BAR HEIGHT

Your weight distribution is also affected by the height of the bars relative to the saddle. Excessively high bars put your weight too far back, compromising the grip from the front wheel. Very low bars put your weight too far forward, making it hard to help the front wheel over obstacles in the trail and causing problems on steep descents. As a starting point, try the bars a couple of inches below the saddle (set at pedaling height).

STEM ADJUSTMENTS

Nearly every modern mountain bike has a handlebar stem that clamps onto the outside of the fork's steerer tube. To adjust the height you need to change the position of the spacers below the stem. If there are no, or insufficient, spacers you'll have to change the stem for one that sits at a different angle.

HANDLEBAR ADJUSTMENTS

The other option is to change the handlebar itself. Bars are available in a wide range of rises – the difference in height between the center of the bar and the ends where the grips are. Watch for the bar angle too – bars have sweep, for the best comfort they need to sweep up as well as back.

POSITIONING THE CONTROLS

The final element of bike setup is positioning the brake and shift levers. These obviously need to be readily accessible for control, but beyond that there are many fine-tuning options that can improve things. Don't over-tighten the bolts on brake levers and shifters – they need to be tight enough to not move in normal use but allow them to move if knocked in a crash.

BRAKE LEVER ANGLE

The angle of the brake lever should be similar to the angle your arm takes to reach the handlebar; your wrists should be as straight and comfortable as possible when they are placed on the bars. This enables the tendons and muscles in your arm to pull in a linear motion, which is the most efficient way. It's worth experimenting with positioning the levers slightly higher than what appears to be the 'natural' position when seated – doing so promotes a dropped-wrist riding position which improves control. Higher levers are also easier to access when your weight is low and back for steep descents, which is when you need the brakes most.

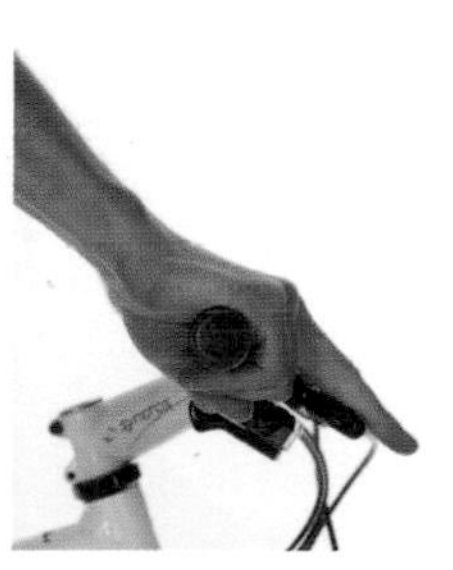

Adjusting the lever angle is simple. There is a 4 or 5mm Allen bolt under the brake lever clamp. Depending on the particular levers and gear shifters used, the bolt can be tricky to access – ball-ended Allen wrenches that can be used at an angle are useful here. Or loosen the shifter first and move that out of the way.

As well as the angle, you can adjust the levers in and out on the bar. Position them so that you can easily reach them with your first two fingers.

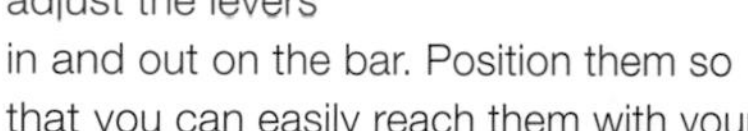

Brake levers are also adjustable for reach – how far away they sit from the grip. This adjustment will either be a small Allen bolt behind the lever or sometimes an obvious tool-free dial.

SHIFTER POSITION

The gear shifters can be adjusted in the same way as the brake levers – loosen pinch bolt, move shifter, retighten. Position them so that you can easily reach the levers – SRAM shifters use only your thumb, Shimano ones use your thumb and first finger. The pods are designed to fit snugly to the brake lever, but be aware that the cable adjuster needs to be accessed easily – so don't rest it where you can't reach it.

The SRAM Matchmaker clamps shown here (Shimano has a similar arrangement) share a single bar clamp between the brake lever and shifter. The shifter can be angled up and down on the clamp and there are also two alternative mounting positions for in and out adjustment.

PEDALS

While many mountain bikers used toe clips and straps on caged pedals in the early days, these are all but extinct now. For most riders, pedal choice comes down to clip-in units (also known, confusingly, as 'clipless' because they did away with toe clips) that use shoe-mounted metal cleats to lock in to a sprung retention mechanism, or flat pedals, with small pins to provide grip on a flat-soled shoe. It's a matter of personal preference – clip-in pedals are more efficient and many riders find the added security helps confidence, but just as many prefer the freedom of movement and ability to quickly bail out of flats.

Pedal maintenance varies, but a lot of pedals use a similar bearing setup to Shimano SPD units and it's these that we look at here.

INSTALLING PEDALS

1 The most important thing to remember about pedals is that pedals have a left- and right-hand thread. Most systems stamp 'L' and 'R' on the axle somewhere so you know which is which. This refers to the side of the bike that the pedal is supposed to go on. On Shimano pedals the stamp is usually on the flat part of the pedal spindle, where the wrench attaches.

2 Pedal threads must be greased. Use a quality waterproof synthetic or an anti-seize grease. Clean the threads and regrease them regularly. Because axles are made out of steel and cranks are made out of aluminum, there can be problems with threads. Be careful not to cross-thread the cranks as they will be ruined.

3 Many cranks come with washers that should be inserted between the pedal and the crank arm. These are designed to prevent fretting damage to the face of the crank from the shoulders of the pedal axle. With carbon fiber and lightweight aluminum cranks, this can lead to failure.

4 The drive-side (right-hand) pedal is a right-hand thread, tightening clockwise in the conventional manner. The non-drive-side (left-hand) pedal is a left-hand thread. This means that both sides tighten toward the front of the bike. The easiest way to remember this is to hold the pedal up to the crank, flat on your fingers, and spin the cranks backward as if you were freewheeling.

5 Tighten the pedals to the manufacturer's recommended torque setting. Hold the opposite crank or the rear wheel and use the added leverage to help you tighten the pedals. To remove the pedals, it is probably easiest if you stand the bike on the floor. You will remove the pedal in the direction of the freewheel, so you may have to hold the opposite crank to prevent it from spinning.

6 As well as wrench flats on the axle, most pedals also have a hexagonal hole for an Allen wrench in the end. This can be accessed from the back of the crank arm. Some lightweight pedals can only be installed and removed this way. Use a long Allen wrench and watch your hands on the chainrings.

PEDAL BEARING SERVICING

There are many different kinds of pedal on the market. We're looking at Shimano SPD units here, as they're the most popular. Some other pedals can be serviced in a similar way.

1 Dry or gritty bearings can be cleaned and regreased, and loose bearings tightened. Binding bearings may suggest a bent axle. Most Shimano pedals use the same replaceable cartridge-style axle. There is a special tool to undo the collars on the pedals.

2 Place the special collar tool in a vice and loosen the pedal (there is an arrow on the pedal collar to show you which direction to turn it). The pedal body can be removed and cleaned thoroughly with degreaser and a toothbrush.

3 With the axle removed, you can assess the damage. Hold the bearing part and spin the axle stub. If it is wobbly and the bearings are very loose, you will probably have to replace the complete assembly. Slight looseness can be adjusted out.

4 Remove the lock nut and the top cone. If the bearings are dull and pitted and the cones have similar pitting and marks, you will be better off replacing the complete unit. You can adjust the cones with this special tool or with the appropriate sized wrenches. It's a very tricky job and it's very easy to lose the 3/32-inch bearings. If you are stripping the axle, you'll need fresh bearings and grease. Readjusting the cones is very similar to adjusting wheel bearings. You are looking to set the collar so it has no play and isn't binding onto the bearings.

5 Before replacing a new axle or the restored old one, pack the pedal body with grease. Don't fill the pedal body right to the top, there needs to be space for the axle to fit back in. Ideally you need slightly more grease than will fit, so a small amount of fresh grease purges the inner bearing as you tighten the axle unit.

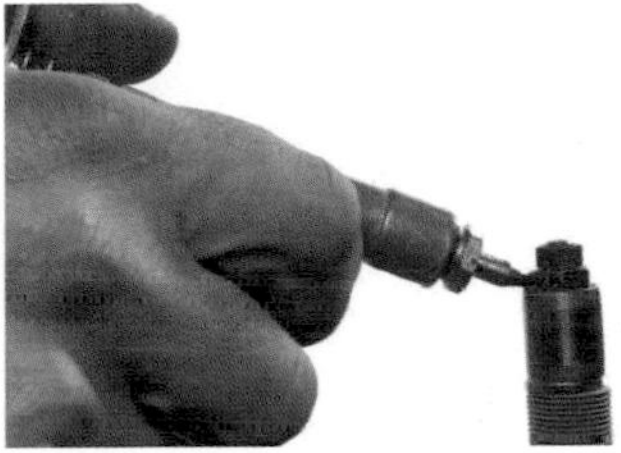

6 Tighten the pedal body onto the axle using the same tool. You only need to tighten it by hand – over-tightening can break the collar and bind the bearings. The pressure of the grease being forced through the bearing can make it hard to turn – if you're really struggling, take out some of the grease from the pedal body and try again.

SPD PEDAL CLEATS

SPD and other clipless pedals use a metal cleat bolted to the sole of the shoe to click into the pedal. You need the appropriate shoes, but all mountain bike pedal systems use the same two-bolt installation. Most shoes come ready to install the cleats, although some will have a rubber cover over the cleat bolts. This may be held in place by bolts through the nuts, or you may have to cut the cover out with a utility knife.

Regular cleaning and lubrication is essential for reliable and consistent performance. In particular, rocks, grit or dried mud around the cleat can prevent it from clicking into the pedal. Pick out any such obstructions. Lubricate the cleats regularly to prevent them from rusting up, as rust will wear the pedal and cleat out more quickly.

1 Prepare the threads in the plates with an anti-seize grease. The bolts will rust pretty quickly and become impossible to remove if you don't. You can replace these screws with stainless steel bolts (you can buy these from an engineering supplier) as they are less likely to rust and will therefore last longer.

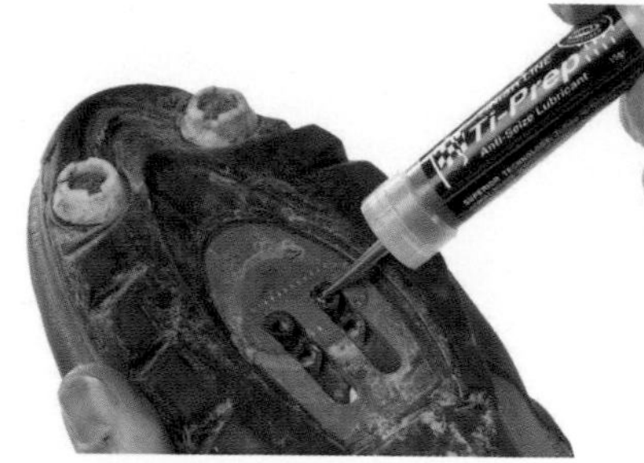

2 Some shoes don't have a built-in threaded plate but require one to be added from the inside. Lift up the part of the insole behind the cleat box and push the plate in so that it fits into the slots in the sole.

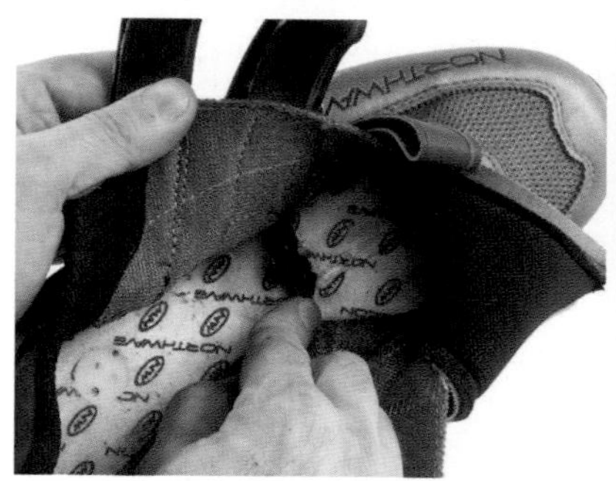

3 Assess the position of the ball of your foot over the pedal axle. Mark on the side of your shoe where the ball of your foot is, then mark a line across the sole of your shoe. Use this reference to decide which set of holes in the plates to use. Check the angle that your feet naturally rest at by sitting on a high stool with your feet dangling. Angle the cleats accordingly.

4 The correct cleat position is with the ball or pushing part of your foot over the pedal axle. This requires measuring and some trial and error to get it right. It's also best to get someone to help you do this job, as you can only adjust the cleat position properly once the cleats are in place.

REMOVING WORN CLEATS

If you applied plenty of grease when you fitted the cleats, they shouldn't be too hard to remove. The main difficulty is that the bolt heads tend to get deformed by walking on rocks, making it hard to engage an Allen wrench sufficiently to undo them. Often simply tapping the Allen wrench in with a hammer is enough to get it past the burrs in the head. Make sure it's well engaged or the head will round out. If all else fails, you'll have to drill the bolt heads out. This is time-consuming as the bolts are very hard. Use progressively larger drill bits until the head pops off. You should then be able to extract the rest of the bolt with pliers.

5 When you're happy with the position of the cleats, tighten the bolts to the recommended torque setting. Alternate between the two bolts, tightening a little at a time. Do not over-tighten them as the threads can strip very easily, in which case you would have to replace the sole insert.

6 Shoes usually come with a sticker to cover the slots in the sole on the inside, both to prevent the shoe plate rubbing on the insole and to stop water coming in. If you don't have the sticker, duct tape works equally well.

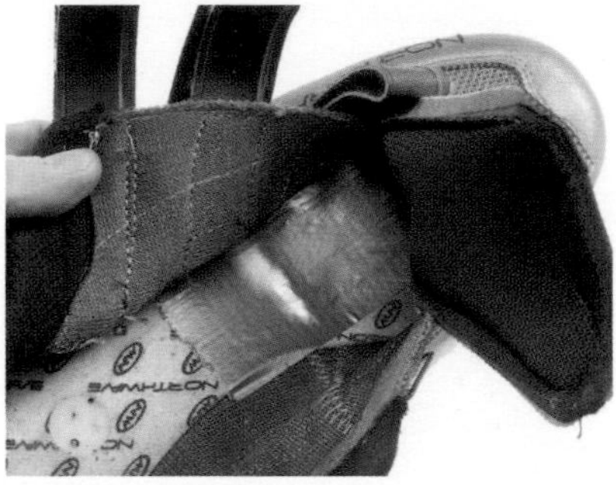

PEDAL TIPS

- Noisy or creaking pedals can be due to worn cleats or simply dry threads. Regrease the threads regularly and replace your cleats before they start to release on their own. It's not only annoying, it can also be dangerous.

- The cleat on the side you release most often when you stop will wear more quickly than the other one, so swap them around for a longer life.

Bicycle wheels are one of the most efficient structures around, deriving enormous strength from lightweight parts. The secret is the spoke tension. Wheels are pre-stressed structures, with loads on the wheel distributed across all the spokes. Without adequate spoke tension, they'd start to fall apart very quickly. The moving parts of wheels need attention too. Hub bearings take a lot of beating, being subject to attack from water, mud, grit and other hostile substances.

REMOVING WHEELS

FRONT WHEELS – QUICK RELEASE

1 Safety tabs are designed to prevent the wheel from falling out should the quick-release (QR) lever be clamped too loosely. Because of the tabs, you'll need to both open the QR lever and undo the nut on the opposite side a little to allow the wheel to come out. Two or three turns is usually enough. The wheel will then drop out.

2 The springs on the inside of the quick-release mechanism help centralize the nut and the lever to push them away from the bike. They also make it easier to replace the wheel, as you don't have to center the assembly. This leaves your hands free to hold the bike and the wheel.

3 The front wheel has to be firmly placed into the dropouts before you can close the lever. Replace the wheels with the bike on the ground. This way the weight of the bike can help make the wheels go in straight.

4 Once the wheel is slotted into the dropouts, slowly tighten the nut until the lever starts to tighten. When the lever is directly in line with the skewer, as shown here, that is enough – this will ensure that the lever will close tightly enough. It should take a firm push to close – if it leaves a mark on a bare hand, it's sufficiently tight. If it's too easy to close, it's too easy to open too.

FRONT WHEELS – THROUGH-AXLE

1 Through-axle systems like the Maxle or QR15 don't have a separate QR skewer. Instead the whole axle comes out. They have a familiar-looking lever on one end, which is the first thing to open. Maxles have the lever on the right, QR15 on the left.

2 Both through-axle systems feature holes in the fork legs rather than open-ended dropouts. This means that the wheel can't fall out, although it could work loose – if you feel any looseness or rattling from the front end, stop and check.

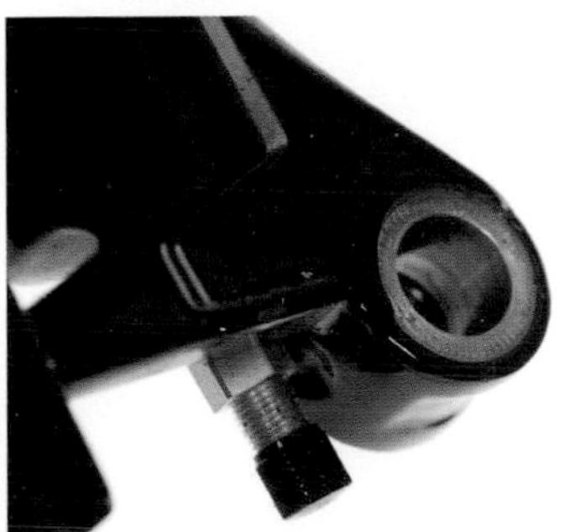

3 With the lever open, you can use it as a handle to unscrew the axle from the threads in the fork. Maxles require the open lever to be engaged in the slot on the end of the axle to unscrew them.

4 Once the axle is disengaged from the threads it will pull straight out. Sometimes they stick in the hub – Maxles stick out on the non-lever side and can be tapped across; if a QR15 axle needs help you'll need a suitable tool to insert into the threaded end before tapping.

5 With the axle out, the wheel will drop out of the forks. The ends of the hub engage in pockets on the inside of the fork legs to ensure good alignment. It can be quite a snug fit between the fork legs – you may have to wiggle it a bit before it comes out.

6 To put the wheel back in, align the brake rotor with the caliper and push the wheel back into the pockets. Reinsert the axle. You need to screw it in until it stops, then tighten the lever. Maxle levers can be tightened to point in any direction. The closing tension can be adjusted using the nut on the opposite end.

7 QR15 levers have to close in the direction they're pointing when tight. This should be either toward the back of the bike or vertically alongside the fork leg. If it's in the wrong place, take it out and remove the small bolt in the threaded insert on the right-hand fork leg.

8 With the bolt removed, the insert can be popped out and reinserted at a different orientation. Use the numbers for reference. The axle will now become tight in a position that lets the lever close in a useful direction.

REAR WHEELS – QUICK RELEASE

1 The chain should be on the smallest sprocket at the back and the largest chainring. This makes it easier to get the chain off the cassette and easier to replace the wheel afterward. Stand behind the bike and hold the bike upright with your legs trapping the wheel, leaving your hands free to remove the wheel. Now undo the lever. Rear dropouts don't have safety tabs because the chain helps to keep the wheel in, so there's no need to undo the nut.

2 The wheel will remain trapped into the bike by the chain, so twist the derailleur backward to release the wheel. The chain should stay on the front chainring, so it will be easier if you start with the chain in this position when you replace the wheel.

3 To replace the rear wheel, the derailleur needs to spring into the correct position with the wheel in the bike. Next, wrap the chain over the top of the smallest sprocket to help the wheel slot into the dropouts. Take care to line the disc brake up equidistant from the pads in the caliper.

4 Pull the wheel upward and backward, and it should slot into place easily. If it doesn't, the wheel may have become snagged on the brake pads or the derailleur may not be in the correct gear position. Close the QR lever, ensuring that it feels tight as it closes.

REAR WHEELS – THROUGH AXLE

1 Through-axle systems are increasingly common on rear wheels, with the most common being a 12mm axle with a hub 142mm wide. There's a version of the Maxle in this size, which works in the same way as the front Maxle. Or you may find an X12 axle, which unscrews from the left-hand side using a 5mm Allen wrench.

2 With the axle removed, the wheel comes out in the same way as with a conventional quick release. Pull the derailleur backward to get the chain and jockey wheels out of the way.

3 Replacing the wheel is the reverse process. As with front through axles, rear systems rely on the ends of the hub engaging in pockets on the frame. You'll need to get the brake rotor lined up with the caliper before the wheel will go fully home.

4 It can take a few tries to get everything lined up on both sides. As with front wheels, it's easiest to do this with the wheel on the ground so that the bike's own weight keeps everything in place.

HUBS

CUP AND CONE BEARINGS

Traditional cup and cone bearing hubs are very simple to service. The first few times can be challenging, but experience really speeds the process up. The key is to make sure that all the components are in top condition – any wear and tear to the cones or bearings means that the parts should be replaced.

Hubs will need a complete service every four to six months depending on weather conditions and how often you ride. Fresh grease and regular adjustment will keep hubs rolling for a long time. Shimano cone hubs are excellent because you can rebuild them very easily and quickly and they use top-quality bearings and hardened steel cones. Look after them properly and they'll last almost indefinitely.

Loose hubs do not last very long. Grab your wheel by the tire and shake the wheel from side to side while it is still in the bike. If you feel a slight knock or "play" through the tire, the hub is loose. This means that the bearings are bashing around inside the hub and slowly disintegrating, and the seals are more exposed, allowing water and muck into the hub. Leave the hub like this and it won't take long for the internal parts to fail completely. Rebuilding the wheel with a new hub is far more costly and time-consuming than replacing the grease and the bearings every few months.

FRONT HUBS

1 The key to easy hub servicing is only working on one side. If you keep one side intact, the spacing over the lock nuts is easier to retain. A standard QR front hub measures 100mm between the faces of the locknuts. This measurement is critical so that the wheel can easily be replaced in the forks. Through-axle hubs are 110mm wide.

2 Cone wrenches are very thin and flat. This means that they can fit into the machined flats on the sides of the cone and can adjust and tighten the cones without snagging on the washer and lock-nut. Use the correct size and don't use cone wrenches to remove your pedals, as this will damage them. Hold the cone with a cone wrench and release the lock nut with a 17mm wrench.

3 Undo and remove the lock nut, then the washer and, finally, the cone. The cone is made from hardened steel and has a highly polished bearing surface. Inspect the cone carefully for any rough patches on the surface, which is known as pitting. On most front wheels there is only a cone, washer and lock nut.

4 Remove the cone, spacers and – very carefully – the axle. It's best to do this over something that will catch the bearings should they fall out. Place the threaded components down on the workbench or over an Allen wrench in the order they came off the hub to help you remember the order to return them. Clean the axle and cones, leaving one side on the axle and in one piece. Keep all the bearings so that you can check you are replacing the same size and quantity.

5 Clean the inside of the bearing surfaces and inspect for damage. If the bearing surfaces and cones are pitted, you will need to replace either the cones or the hub assembly. Replacing the cones and the bearings and resetting them in grease will usually solve any hub roughness.

6 You don't have to remove the hub seals – they're factory fitted and are very hard to replace properly as they are pressed into the shell of the hub, and it is possible to see into the hub with the seals in place. However, if you do have to remove them, be very careful. Wrap a rag around a tire lever and pry the seals out carefully. Don't use a screwdriver as they can bend the seal, and if that happens you'll never get it back in again. To replace the seal, use your fingers to locate it and then tap it home using a rubber mallet.

7 It is good practice to replace the bearings after every strip down. The bearings are slightly more vulnerable than the cones and the hub surfaces, so they tend to wear out first. Look at them closely and you will see tiny potholes. Bearings need to be mirror finished, so if they are even slightly dull they need replacing. It's useful to have a magnetic screwdriver for this job, as it makes re-installation far easier. Store spare bearings on a magnet to make them easier to manage.

8 When all the bearings are installed, take the loose cone and push it back into the hub. Rotate it a couple of times to seat the bearings. This will also tell you if there is any damage to the bearing surface inside the hub, and will stick the bearings in place so you can turn the wheel over to do the other side. Next, double-check that there are the right amount of bearings in the hub. Lastly, smear a little more grease on top of the bearings and check there isn't any grease inside the hub. You will then be able to push the axle through without making a big mess.

9 Replace the axle (remember to return it in the same way it was removed). As you have only disturbed one set of bearings, the spacing will not have been altered. Screw the cone onto the axle and up to the bearings. Spin the axle in your fingers and 'rock' it slightly from side to side – you are looking for the point at which there is no 'play', only smooth spinning. When you are happy that the bearings are running smoothly, replace the washer and then the lock nut. At this stage they need to be finger tight.

10 With practice, you will be able to set the cones like this and simply install the cone as in step 2. However, when you tighten the lock nut for the last time, you may also either loosen the cone slightly or tighten it. Mountain bike hubs have seals in the hub body that will drag a little when the cone is set. To set the cones properly you will need two cone wrenches (13mm for front hubs); with two wrenches you can work the cones against each other. So, if you over-tighten the lock nut, place the two cone wrenches on either side of the hub and slightly undo the cones until the axle spins freely.

REAR HUBS

Much of the information in the front hub section (see pages 85-88) applies to rear hubs too. The bearings are assembled in the same way, although many of the dimensions are different. Rear hubs also contain the freehub mechanism, which can be replaced.

If both cones need to be replaced, it is worth measuring the position of the lock nut and cones before you start work. Measure the distance from the end of the axle to the side of the first lock nut. Then, when you start to remove the cones, work on one side at a time and place the components down in the order that they are removed. Thread them over a screwdriver or an Allen wrench in reverse order so they don't get mixed up.

Before you start, remove the cassette as described on pages 44-45.

1 Work on the non-drive side first. Remove the rubber cover and undo the lock nut. As with the front hub, leave the drive side intact to ensure that the spacing remains identical – this is especially important with the rear hub as uneven spacing can affect the chainline and the gear shifting.

2 As with the front hubs, put all the axle components to one side and clean the hub bearing surfaces. When the hub is cleaned, remove the cassette body with a 10mm Allen wrench. The cassette body is usually factory installed and tight, so you will need an appropriate Allen wrench (a long one). You may need to use a pipe for a little extra leverage to undo the bolt.

3 The bolt that retains the cassette body can be fully removed and the cassette body can be replaced if necessary. To re-install, locate the cassette body on the splines on the end of the hub. Be careful not to lose the washer that sits on the inside of the body. Set the torque wrench to 34.3–49Nm and tighten the bolt.

4 Grease and reset the bearings into the hub. Nine 1/4in bearings are usually required, but, as with the front hub, double-check that you are returning the same amount as you removed. It is impossible to detect damage to the surface of the bearings, so new ones must be used to ensure smooth running. Take your time and set the bearings in grease so that they are covered and the grease is worked in.

5 The grease will be enough to hold the bearings in place. Insert the axle, with the drive-side spacers and cones still in place, from the drive side. It is best to do this over the bench in case the bearings decide to escape.

6 Spin the non-drive side cone onto the axle until it's finger tight. Add any spacers and washers and finally the lock nut, then set the cones. This is harder with the rear hub because the drive-side cone is tucked into the cassette body. It is therefore far easier to do this job with the wheel secured in an axle vice, and some mechanics even adjust the hub when it is back in the bike. However, this requires experience. Lastly, return any rubber covers and you will then be able to re-install the cassette.

CARTRIDGE BEARINGS

Unlike adjustable cup and cone style hubs, cartridge bearing hubs rely on a sealed bearing unit that can be removed and replaced. The bearings are set into a hardened steel cartridge that press-fits into the hub shell or freehub body. This unit is packed with grease and sealed with plastic or labyrinth seals. The quality is determined by the number of bearings and amount of grease packed into them. Once the bearing is pushed into the hub, the axle can be pushed tightly into the bearings. This gives you a smooth spinning feel, as there is less chance of over-tightening the bearing with lock nuts and cones.

The obvious advantage of sealed bearings is that they require less adjustment and servicing than standard cup and cone bearings. However, they are only as good as the quality of bearings and standard of engineering of the hub shells. A cartridge hub at the cheaper end of the range may have push-fit covers and less sealing than a Shimano cup and cone hub.

Sealed bearings do not like side loads and can be easily damaged, so always treat them with care and always use the manufacturer's recommended tools to remove them.

The following method for installing new bearings in hubs with cartridge units is fairly straightforward. Each manufacturer will have its own tools and bearings, but the general principle is fairly standard.

1 The spacers at the end of each side of the axle are either push-fit or locked into place with a threaded lock ring. Sometimes a grub screw can lock them in place. The ones shown here require an Allen wrench and a cone wrench to undo the cassette-retaining spacer.

2 This non-drive-side spacer threads onto the axle end. Many (like Hope) are a simple push-on installation. The key here is the quality of the fit between the axle and the bearing, as this is what takes the strain. Oversize axles are a good idea with sealed bearings as they can handle much more abuse and tend to twist less under load.

3 With the spacers and lock nuts removed, the cassette body can be taken off. On most cartridge hubs the cassette will be a push-fit secured by the drive-side spacer. However, some, like this Bontrager wheel, use a Shimano-type freewheel that is bolted to the hub body. You will need a 10mm Allen wrench to remove this.

4 Push out the old cartridge bearings. This Bontrager wheel's axle has to be tapped out with a plastic mallet. Once one side has been removed, the cartridge will pop out, still attached to the axle.

5 This Bontrager hub has a bolt-on cassette body and is removed in the same way as a Shimano hub (see step 3) with a 10mm Allen wrench. You can see the collar that holds the cartridge bearing. This needs to be cleaned thoroughly before a new bearing can be installed.

6 The remaining bearing on the axle can be tapped off by placing the axle in a die. This allows you to use the axle to remove the remaining bearing on the other side of the hub. To replace the bearing you will have to place it on top of the die and tap the axle back in. When it is flush to the shoulder in the center of the axle, it is ready to be re-installed to the hub.

7 The new bearings can be replaced. All sealed bearings have a code number and can be bought at most engineering suppliers or your local bike shop.

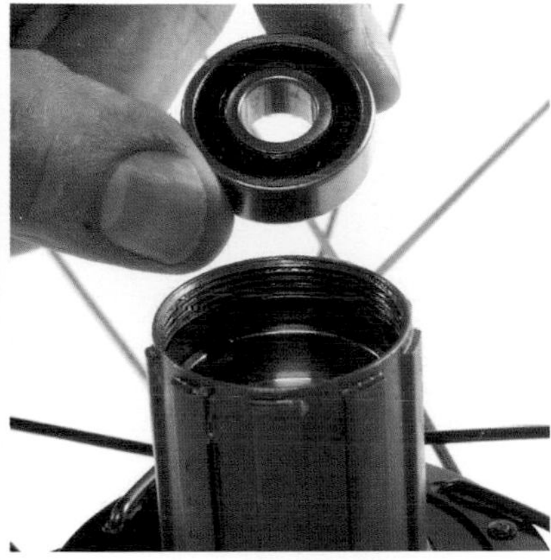

8 Use an appropriate die to seat the new bearings into the hub. They are a tight fit, but must be installed gently so as not to damage the bearing unit or the seals. Press in the new bearings with care. Put some grease around the outside of the bearing and place it square onto the hub. Use an insertion tool that is the same size as the outer part of the bearing. Any side load onto the plastic seal part of the bearing will ruin it. Tap the bearing home.

9 Most cartridge bearing hubs have their own type of cassette. They usually pull off once the lock rings and spacers have been removed. Inside the hub is a series of teeth and on the cassette body are three sprung pawls. These pawls engage with the teeth when you pedal and 'click' around freely when you stop pedaling. The hub pictured here has one circular spring that holds the pawls in place.

10 Here you can see the serrated part inside the hub. This needs to be completely cleaned out and lightly greased before you replace the rebuilt cassette body.

11 Carefully remove the pawls and clean all the dirty grease off the cassette body. Use a toothbrush to clean out all the pawl indentations and spring channels.

12 The cassette shown here has a single circular spring, so the pawls need to be set in grease and then have the spring replaced over them. This does take time as it's quite tricky. Many hubs have springs for individual pawls. If these fail they will need to be replaced as they can get stuck into the serrated parts and ruin the freewheel.

13 Use a light-weight grease on the freehubs. Heavy grease tends to drag inside the hub, which can make the chain sag. To replace the cassette body you will need to push the pawls into the cassette body so it can fit into the hub. Some hubs supply a tool for this. Once the pawls are tucked away, the cassette body should pop into place. Double-check that it rotates freely before you rebuild the rest of the hub.

CARTRIDGE BEARING TIPS

- With care, the seals can be removed with a scalpel blade and the old grease flushed out with degreaser. Use a grease gun to inject fresh grease into the bearings inside the collars.
- Avoid solvent-based lubricants on sealed bearing hubs as they can damage the seals and flush out the grease from the bearings.

Tires are one of the fundamental bike parts. You can do without gears or suspension, but you won't get far without tires. Your tires have to transfer all your inputs to the ground. The rear tire has to use your pedaling efforts to push the bike along. The front tire has to deal with most of the braking and steering. We expect our tires to work in a spectacular range of conditions, from wet and muddy to dry and dusty. While the differences between tires can be subtle, there are certainly differences, and a bad choice could spoil your ride. With no moving parts, the maintenance requirements of tires are relatively minimal. Keep them clean and correctly inflated and check them carefully for rips, tears or excessive wear. The main issue you're likely to face is, of course, punctures.

REMOVING A TIRE

Most tubed tires can be removed without the use of tire levers, although sometimes you'll encounter a really tight combination of tire and rim that just won't shift any other way. Tubeless-ready rims and tires are usually a tighter fit, and if you're using a tubeless conversion that relies on a thick rim tape to seal the spoke holes you may find that that makes things more difficult too. Out on the trail, with potentially cold, wet hands, it's often easier to use levers – see page 116 for trailside tire removal.

1 If you've had a puncture the tire will be flat already, but take the valve cap off and compress the valve core to let any remaining air out. If the tire is fully inflated the air will come out quite quickly. Remove the valve lock ring. Work around the tire and pop the beads inward from the rim.

2 Starting opposite the valve, squeeze the tire beads together and push them right down into the well of the rim. By pushing them down on one side of the rim you should be able to get enough slack to push the beads off at the opposite side of the rim.

3 Work your hands outward, pushing the slack in the tire around the rim with your thumbs. Keep the pressure on so that you're pulling the top bit of the tire into the rim. It helps to rest the top edge of the rim against your legs to keep the tire pushed in.

4 When your hands meet at the opposite side of the wheel, the beads should be clear of the lip of the rim and can be pulled off. If they're not quite there, try the procedure again. You may have to resort to tire levers – often just one will do it.

5 Once you've got a few inches of bead clear, run a tire lever (or finger, but take care in case there are thorns or glass in there) around the rest of the bead to lift it off thc rim. Once one bead is off it's usually easy to pop the other one off.

6 Remove the inner tube. Make sure you check the inside of the tire thoroughly for thorns before putting a new or repaired inner tube in. It's annoying to repair a puncture only for it to go flat again instantly.

PATCHING AN INNER TUBE

1 Find the hole. This is usually a case of pumping up the tube and listening. Just keep pumping until you hear the hiss. Failing that, pump the tube up and look closely at it all the way around – you might not see the hole but you'll feel the air coming out. Really tiny holes might only be discovered by dunking the tube in a bowl of water. Once you find the hole, place your finger and thumb over it as you don't want to lose it.

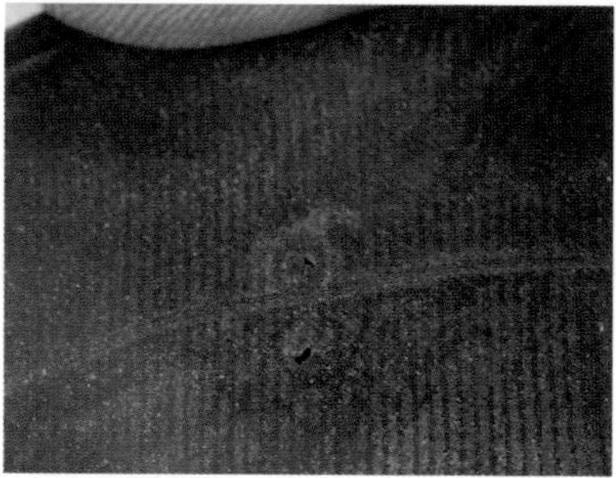

2 Roughen up the area around the hole with some sandpaper. This will help the glue penetrate the rubber and ensure the patch adheres properly. The glue is a contact adhesive (it works when the patch is placed on it), but needs to be applied to a grease-free and dry tube in order to work properly.

3 Apply plenty of glue to the area, starting at the hole and working outward. Keep an eye on where the hole is so you can get the patch over it properly later on. Leave the glue for five minutes until it is almost completely dry.

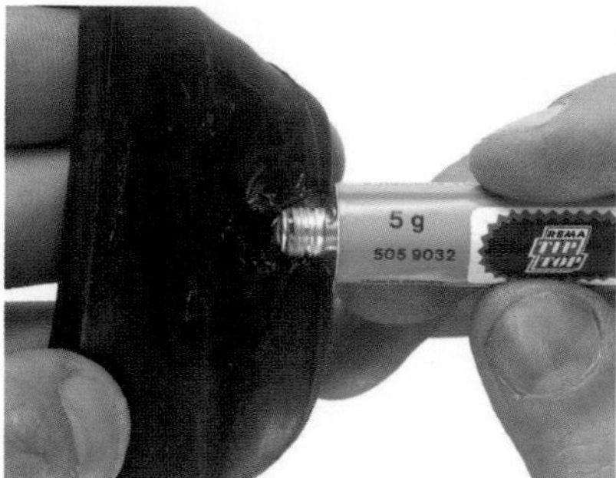

4 Most fixable holes can be covered by a 2cm patch. If it's a pinch flat use two patches (one over each hole) rather than one big one. Apply firm pressure to the patch with your thumb, as you want the patch to be fully in place before you re-inflate. To guarantee good adhesion, put something heavy on the patch and leave it for a while.

5 Remove the plastic backing film from the center. It's usually perforated in the middle and will split if you bend the tube. Don't pull it off from a corner as it can pull the patch off with it. The backing is used to make sure you don't touch the underside of the patch and so you can press it onto the tube easily.

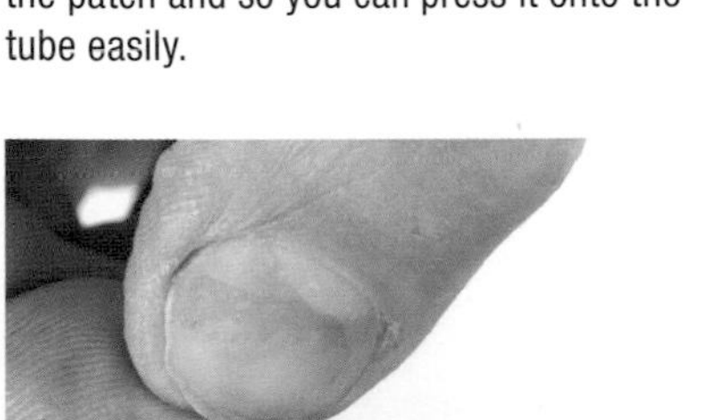

6 If you can dust the area with talc, this will prevent the glue from sticking to the inside of the tire casing and help it slide into place as you inflate the tire. It's good practice to lightly dust the whole tube with talc so it can move slightly inside the tire.

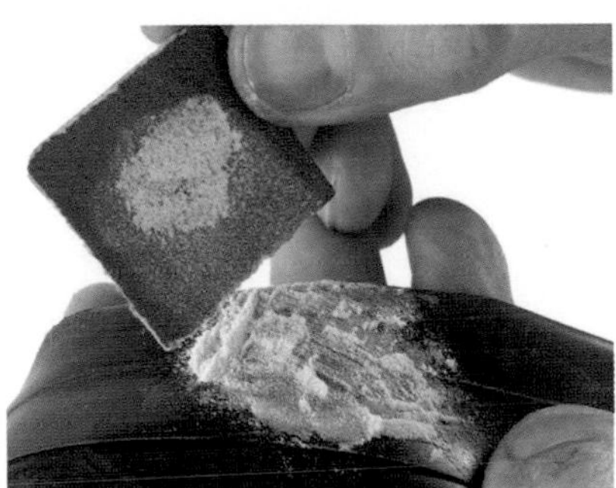

PUTTING ON THE TUBE AND TIRE

1 Put one tire bead onto the rim, taking careful note of the orientation of the tire – if there are directional arrows on it, make sure they're going the right way. Allow the bead to sit in the well of the rim.

2 Pump the inner tube up just enough for it to hold its shape so it's less likely to get pinched. Push the valve through the hole in the rim and pop the partially inflated tube into the tire all the way around.

3 Starting opposite the valve, hook the other bead into the rim. The procedure is very similar to taking the tire off – apply pressure around the tire, engaging the bead as you go and trying to generate enough slack to pop the last bit on.

4 By the time your hands meet at the far side of the tire, you should be able to push the last bit of bead over the rim with your thumbs. If it's almost there but not quite, work around from the valve side again. Very snug tires may need some encouragement from a tire lever.

5 Replace the locking nut on the valve stem. Undo the small locking tip of the valve (Presta type only). Free it up by pressing it in a couple of times; this will enable the valve to pass air in easily as sometimes it gets 'stuck' after full inflation.

6 Push the pump head firmly onto the valve. Sometimes you will have to place a thumb behind the tire to prevent the valve vanishing into the hole as you push it home (some valves have lock rings to prevent this).

7 All good pumps have a locking lever. This ensures that the pump head makes an airtight seal over the valve and means you can concentrate on inflating the tire. Valve cores can be removed and replaced as they wear out. The seal can also be turned around to cope with either valve type (see your pump instructions as this depends on the make).

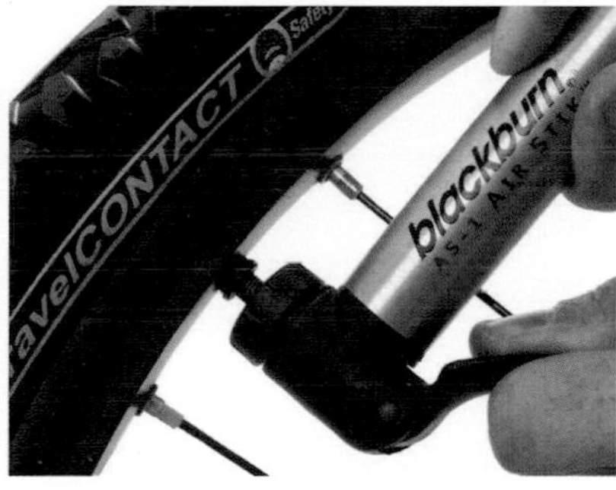

8 Pump firmly but don't rush. If you push too hard or at an awkward angle you can bend the valve or snap the locking part off. Use all of the pumping stroke and take your time. Make sure there's adequate air pressure in the tire before riding it again. Some tires need inflating to their maximum pressure to properly seat themselves on the rim – deflate them slightly again from there for riding.

TROUBLESHOOTER

If the tire is leaking rapidly, check the following:

- Gashes in the sidewall, even if they don't go through the tire completely, can leak slowly and will reduce the performance of the tire. Have a good look around the whole tire and patch any that may seem suspect.
- Check the bead seating. Inflate the tire to 10 per cent more than the maximum recommended pressure. Then deflate the tire completely. The bead should remain firmly tucked into the rim edge and retain the seal. If it doesn't, the bead may be damaged.
- Clean the rim and bead with soapy water and replace the tire as recommended.
- Check the rims for dents or scratches.
- Lastly, if these tips don't help, inflate the tire to about 50 PSI and submerge it in the bath. Any holes will show up pretty quickly.

TUBELESS TIRES

INSTALLING TUBELESS TIRES

1 UST double-walled rims are sealed, with no access to the spoke nipples through the inside of the rim. The nipples are oversized and thread directly into the rim. This means you will have to true the wheel with this special spoke key, but also means that you can replace a spoke without having to remove the tires.

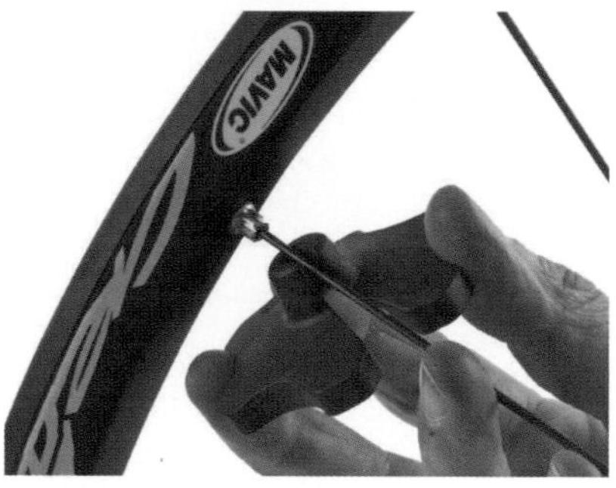

2 UST tires are a little heavier than standard tires, with a more substantial sidewall and a fatter bead. As with a standard tire you will need to check the direction arrows on the side wall. You must only use ETRTO-compatible tires, but most of the main manufacturers have a UST option to their product lines. Tubeless-ready tires with sealant are a lighter option.

3 The valve is the key element to the tubeless wheel. It's recommended that you replace the valve periodically. This valve is for a sealed rim – some tubeless-ready rims require a rim tape with a built-in valve, and a similar arrangement is used for tubeless conversion kits.

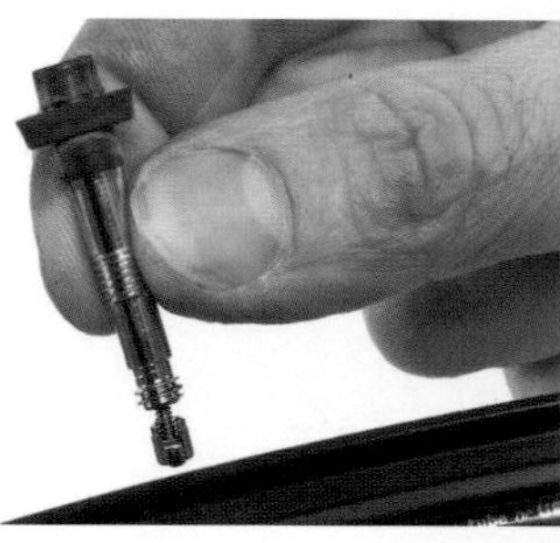

4 The rubber flange of the valve has to sit inside the well in the middle of the rim. A little soapy water or Vaseline on the rubber seal will help seal the valve and the rim. Here you can see the well that runs around the base of the rim – this helps to install the tire bead. Also notice the absence of spoke holes.

5 There is an O-ring that fits over the valve to seal it to the rim. Check that this is in place over the join between the rim and the valve, and replace it on a regular basis. Moisten it slightly with some Vaseline to help it seal the air in completely.

6 The lock ring is tightened on top of the O-ring. This should only be screwed on finger tight. It is possible to fit a Schrader valve adaptor to the Presta-size valve, but the UST system can only be used with the UST valve. Some valves for tubeless-ready systems have removable cores to allow sealant to be injected through them.

7 Soap the rim with some very diluted soapy water. Then, starting opposite the valve hole, place one side of the tire bead over the rim and into the well in the middle of the rim. If you push the bead into this well, it makes it far easier to pull the tire onto the rim as it adds some slack to the bead. Work with both hands around the rim toward the valve hole. Do not be tempted to use tire levers; the tire should go on with minimal force.

8 Once one side of the tire is on, push the bead to the side of the well so that there's space for the other bead. Run your finger around the well inside the rim and push the bead firmly toward the other side of the rim. Then, starting opposite the valve hole again, insert the second bead, forcing it into the well again so that once you reach the valve hole there will be enough slack to pull the tire on easily.

9 Pulling the final bit on is tricky, so be careful not to damage the tire bead at this point. You may have to force the tire on a little, but if the bead has been placed into the well correctly it should be pretty easy. If the tire is too tight, work both sides of the wheel around to the valve hole until there is a small amount left to pull on. You may need to add a little more soapy water to assist this bit.

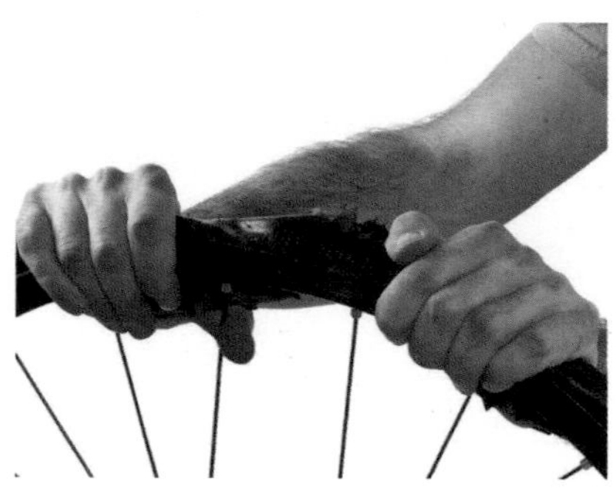

10 If you're using a tubeless-ready tire and the valve core isn't removable, add sealant directly into the tire before engaging the last part of the bead. You don't need much – 40-100g should be ample. Tire sealant is latex based, with various different added ingredients depending on the brand.

11 It should be possible to inflate a tubeless setup with an ordinary floor pump, although you may have to be quick with the first few pumps. The theory is that there'll be a good enough seal between the tire and the rim bed to hold sufficient air pressure to force the beads out to the bead locks on the rim. Keep pumping until the tire pops into the rim.

12 If air comes out as fast as you can put it in, try a bit more soapy water and make sure the tire is on the rim evenly all the way around. You may need to use a compressor, or pop a tube in just to engage the beads – once they've 'popped', release one side sufficiently to get the tube out. With one bead engaged it should be easier to get the other one to go. Once the beads are engaged, adjust air pressure as desired.

09 SUSPENSION AND STEERING

The purpose of mountain bike suspension is twofold. First, by isolating the rider from bumps, comfort is improved and fatigue reduced. Second, suspension maintains contact between the wheels and the ground, improving traction and control. All bike suspension is adjustable to a degree, and some systems are adjustable to the point of bewilderment. Suspension needs to be adjusted based not only on your weight but also to accommodate different riding styles. A racer is likely to run suspension harder and with faster rebound than a recreational rider, who's likely to be more interested in comfort. In this book we won't be going into the nuances of each particular suspension configuration, as there are too many of them and they are constantly changing in terms of design and setup. So instead we will concentrate on the fundamentals of any suspension setup: spring rate and damping.

FRONT FORK SET-UP

Nearly every mountain bike has a suspension fork. There are plenty of fully rigid bikes out there if you want one, but you have to seek them out. While a suspension fork has substantial benefits for most riders, if you don't set it up correctly it'll be a liability.

1 Most forks have an O-ring on one of the stanchions that shows how much the fork has compressed. If there isn't one, wrap a small zip tie around the stanchion. Push the O-ring or zip tie down until it touches the fork wiper seal. If your fork has a lock-out lever, make sure it's disengaged.

2 Prop yourself up against a wall with your elbow, or ask for help to hold the bike upright, and sit on the bike in the normal riding position with your usual riding outfit (including a pack if you normally ride with one). If you've compressed the fork a lot when getting on the bike, you will need to reach down and reset the O-ring. You are looking to spread your weight without bouncing on the saddle or pedals.

3 Being careful not to compress the fork further, climb off the bike and measure the sag directly from the fork leg. Sag should be between a quarter and a third of the total travel available. For example, on a 120mm fork you should look for sag of 30-40mm.

4 If you have air-sprung forks there'll be an air valve on them somewhere – on RockShox and Fox forks it's on top of the left-hand leg. Remove the threaded cap to access the valve. If you have a coil-sprung fork, you should find a preload dial in the same place.

5 Use a shock pump to adjust the air pressure in the fork. If the fork has too much sag, add air. If it doesn't sag enough, let air out using the release valve on the pump. Make adjustments 5psi at a time then repeat steps 1-3. If you have a coil fork, turn the preload dial counter-clockwise for more sag, clockwise for less sag.

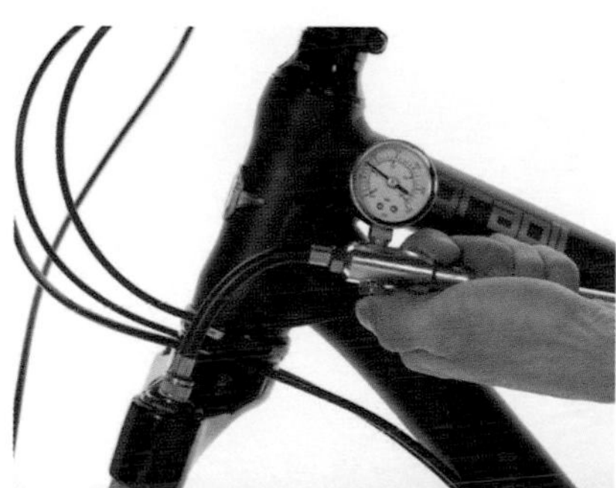

6 Some forks have a separate 'negative spring' that balances the main spring at rest for better performance on small bumps. Set this to the same pressure as the main spring – you can adjust it a little either way to suit your preferred feel.

DAMPING ADJUSTMENTS

Most forks (except very cheap models) have some form of adjustable damping. The most common adjustment is rebound damping, which controls how quickly the fork returns to its rest position after hitting a bump. As a very rough rule of thumb, push hard and quickly down on the bars with flat hands and then lift your hands up as quickly as possible. The bars should keep pace with your hands – adjust the rebound damping to suit.

REAR SHOCK SET-UP

Most rear shocks are air sprung. As well as being lighter than coil-sprung shocks, they're also more adjustable, simply by adding or removing air. Air shocks can deal with riders across a very wide range of weights. If you have a coil shock, adjust the sag using the preload collar. If there isn't sufficient range of adjustment you'll need to change the spring for a softer or harder one.

1 Before starting the setup process, make sure any lockout levers or platform damping adjusters are off or at the minimum setting. You need to have only the air spring supporting your weight.

2 Push the shock O-ring up the shock body so that it contacts the air canister. The O-ring will be forced along the shock as it compresses, showing you how much travel you've used.

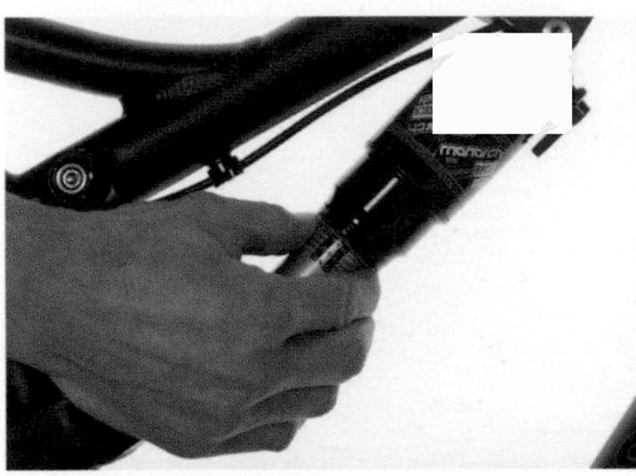

3 Propping yourself up against a wall with your elbow, sit on the bike in your normal riding position and usual riding outfit (including pack if you use one). You'll probably need to reset the O-ring once the shock has settled.

4 Being careful not to compress the shock further, climb off the bike and measure the sag directly from the shock body. Some shocks, like the RockShox unit pictured, have a sag scale etched onto the shaft so you won't need a tape measure.

5 In general, you're looking for 25-35% of the available travel as sag. As an example, if your shock has 50mm of stroke you're aiming for about 12-17mm of sag. The ideal settings vary with different rear suspension designs, so consult your owner's manual – there's usually a suggested measurement there.

6 Use a shock pump to add or remove air until you've got the suggested sag setting. A higher pressure gives less sag, a lower air pressure gives more sag. Shock pumps have a pressure gauge – make a note of the correct pressure when you've got the sag right.

7 Adjust the rebound damping in a similar way to the front fork. A good rule of thumb is to ride off a curb – the rear suspension should compress, extend slightly past the rest position and then settle back to it.

BASIC HEADSET ADJUSTMENT

1 To check the headset, apply the front brake and rock the bike backward and forward. You will feel or hear a slight knocking if the unit is loose. If you're not sure, rest your hand across the fork crown and bottom headset cup to feel any movement directly. Sometimes worn suspension fork bushings can knock too, but you can isolate the headset bearings by performing the test with the wheel turned 90°.

2 Undo the (usually two) bolts on the side of the stem. These bolts clamp the stem to the top of the steerer tube. As well as connecting the stem to the steerer so that you can steer, fixing the stem maintains the correct preload on the headset bearings.

3 Once you have loosened the clamp bolts, tighten the top cap slightly to take up any play in the system. You will only need a small nudge to tighten the unit (to around 3Nm). If the headset has sealed cartridge bearings you'll be able to feel when the headset is tight. With loose bearings it's a little harder – be careful not to over-tighten the top cap.

4 If the top cap bolt becomes hard to turn but the headset is still loose, it's possible that the top cap has bottomed out on the fork steerer. The top of the steerer needs to be 2-3mm below the top of the stem to work properly. If the steerer is flush with the stem, add an extra thin spacer – it can go on top of the stem to leave the bar height unchanged.

HEADSET MAINTENANCE

1 Before removing anything, secure the fork to the frame with a toe strap or zip tie. When the stem and top cap are removed, only friction in the bearings will hold the fork into the frame and it's likely to fall out without anything else to stop it. This could damage the fork, or your foot.

2 Unbolt the front brake caliper from the fork. The front brake hose links the fork and bars, so you need to remove the caliper to be able to completely detach the fork. Loop the hose around the bars to keep it out of the way.

3 It's a good idea to prepare a clean surface to lay all the headset parts on as they come off to avoid confusion. Undo the top cap bolt and remove cap, bolt and any spacers above the stem. At this point the fork is still held in by the stem.

4 Loosen the stem clamp bolts and slide the stem and bars off the steerer. It's fine to let the bars hang from the frame by the gear cables and brake hoses, although you might want to protect the frame with a rag.

5 Lift off the upper bearing cover. There will be a tapered washer helping to hold this in place which can get stuck. Loosen or remove the toe strap and give the steerer a tap with a rubber mallet. If that doesn't work, give it a tap back up. Alternate down and up taps until the washer comes free.

6 You should now be able to slide the fork out of the frame, leaving the upper bearing in its cup. The lower bearing will either stay in its cup or come out on the fork steerer. The bearings will be either a sealed cartridge or loose ball bearings. Loose bearings can be cleaned and regreased.

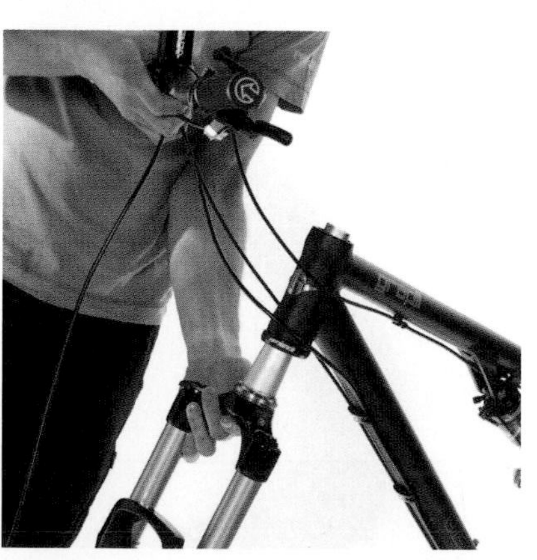

7 Cartridge bearings can simply be removed and replaced if necessary, with a light smear of grease on the outside of the housing to stop them getting stuck in the cups. Make sure that the bearings run smoothly and check the condition of the bearing seals.

8 Re-install the forks, making sure that all the bearings, seals, covers, washers and spacers are in the right order. Tapered systems make this slightly easier because it's impossible to get the bearings in the wrong cups. Re-install the stem, bars and top cap and adjust the headset as per "Basic headset adjustment."

10 ON THE TRAIL

No matter how meticulous your maintenance, there's always the possibility of something going wrong out on the trail. Vigilant checking and tuning will prevent a lot of failures, but it won't stop you from crashing or getting a puncture. Self-sufficiency is part of mountain biking – if you're out in the wilderness and something on your bike breaks, it's up to you to figure it out and get home.

CHANGING A TUBE

Punctures are the single most common mechanical issue encountered during rides. We described how to patch a punctured inner tube in Chapter 8, but you don't want to be patching tubes by the side of the trail especially if it's wet or cold. If you get a puncture, it's best to change the tube and patch the old one at your leisure later on. You may also need to install a tube on the trail even if you use tubeless tires. Any hole too big for sealant to deal with will need a tube to get you home.

1 As soon as you realize you have a flat, stop. It's better to start fixing the flat than trying to ride any further on a potentially hazardous wheel. Riding with a flat can also damage the rim should you hit anything hard on the trail and is likely to damage the tire too. Stopping immeidately may also allow you to find the hole in the tire and remove any sharp objects that may have become trapped in the tread. Remove the wheel and either lay the bike down or hang it from a suitable branch. See page 80 for more on removing wheels.

2 Most mountain bike tires are quite loose fitting and it's usually possible to remove them without tire levers, or with just one (although it's a good idea to carry two or three). Let any remaining air out of the tire and remove the nut from the valve. Work around the tire and push the bead inward away from the rim walls. Starting opposite the valve, push the beads down into the well of the rim, working the resulting slack around the wheel. By the time you get around to the valve side there should be enough slack to pop the bead over the edge of the rim (see chapter 8 for fuller explanations).

3 If you can't get the tire off without tire levers (tubeless tires can be a very tight fit), try using a single one first. Push the tire away from the rim to reveal the bead, slip the lever tip under the bead and pry it over the edge of the rim. Then run the lever around the rim to remove one side of the tire. If you can't pop enough bead over the rim with one lever, try two. Hook them both under the bead but lever with one first, then the other. The second lever will be harder to pull.

4 Whichever method you use, there's no need to remove the tire completely. You just need to pull one bead off the rim so you can remove the inner tube. Push the valve back up through the hole and pull the tube out from inside the tire. Pack it away for repair later.

5 Then check the inside of the tire for thorns or other pointy objects. Carefully run a gloved hand around the inside of the tire – you'll be able to feel anything significant. Leaving the tire on the rim can help you to find whatever caused the puncture. If you can find the hole in the tube and the tire hasn't moved on the rim, you can use the position of the hole to track down the culprit. Use the position of the valve on the tube and the valve hole in the rim as a reference.

6 Self-adhesive patches are useful for trail repairs if you've run out of tubes, but they're not as effective as glued-on patches. If you find a large gash or split in the tire (most likely to be in the sidewall) you'll need to use a tire boot inside the tire to stop the inner tube bulging out. Proper self-adhesive boots are available, but you can improvise with duct tape, cardboard or energy bar wrappers. Whatever you use is only a temporary fix – torn sidewalls mean a new tire.

7 Having identified and remedied the cause of the puncture, you're safe to install a new inner tube. Slightly inflate the replacement tube with a couple of strokes of a mini-pump, just enough for the tube to take shape. Next, insert the valve into the valve hole. Make sure that the valve is seated properly into the rim, then push the tire over the top of the tube. Work the tube carefully into the casing of the tire.

8 Now, start to return the tire bead into the rim. Start opposite the valve hole and work the tire either side with two hands. Push the tire beads right down into the well of the rim to produce enough slack to pull the last part of the tire on by hand. This can be a bit of a struggle depending on the rim and tire model. However, it is best to pull it on this way as using a tire lever can pinch the tube as you lever it on.

9 Once the tire is back on the rim, check that the beads are all in place and that the inner tube isn't pinched between tire and rim. Pump the tire up to the recommended pressure. If the tire doesn't run true (it wobbles as you spin the wheel) re-seat it by letting most of the air out and pulling the tire away from the bead. This will help the bead sit into the rim and usually 'pops' the tire into place.

10 Re-install the wheel in the bike, making sure that the quick-release skewer or through axle system is securely tightened. Give the wheel a spin to check that the brakes aren't rubbing. If they are, the wheel may not be in exactly straight.

TOP 10 TRAIL FAILS (AND HOW TO FIX THEM)

1 PUNCTURES

Cause: A fact of life if you ride off-road. Thorns, sharp rocks and other trail debris can all cause punctures.
Prevention: Run tires at their recommended pressures. Check tire treads for anything that could work through the tire and cause a flat. Replace tires regularly.
Trail fix: Carry spare tubes and a puncture kit. If you are really stuck, tie a tight knot in the tube on either side of the hole, which might get you home.

2 TIRE DISASTERS

Cause: Gashes from rocks or the brake block rubbing on the tire.
Prevention: Check tires for wear and replace regularly. Run tires at their recommended pressures.
Trail fix: Use a tire boot to patch the inside of the tire. You can also use big puncture patches and stiff cardboard.

3 BROKEN CHAIN

Cause: Twisting strain on links of the chain, usually in combination with a very worn or badly installed chain.
Prevention: Use a quality chain, check for wear often and replace it regularly. Don't use gears with extreme crossovers (big ring to big sprocket) and ease pressure when shifting.
Trail fix: Carry a SRAM Powerlink, which will work with most chains.

4 BROKEN SPOKES

Cause: Usually uneven tension in the spokes, which normally happens when the wheel is reaching the end of its life.
Prevention: Regular checkups with a competent wheelbuilder, and having good wheels built in the first place with regular tension.
Trail fix: Folding 'cable spokes' are available, which can fold into a tool kit.

5 RIM/WHEEL FAILURE

Cause: Crashes, poor build, loose spokes and big hits. Rims can wear through and the bead can detach from the rim, which can be catastrophic!
Prevention: Look for wear and dents in the rim and check spoke tension.
Trail fix: Wobbles can be rectified with a spoke wrench, bigger distortions can be pushed out with brute force, but only if a spoke wrench can't do the job.

6 GEAR CABLE FAILURE

Cause: Forcing the gear to shift, or simple wear and tear.
Prevention: Keep the cables lubricated and free-running. Replace cables (including housing) regularly.
Trail fix: The gear stops can be adjusted to run in a suitable single gear to get you home, or you can clamp the cable under a bottle boss bolt. Or carry a spare.

7 BRAKE CABLE / HOSE FAILURE

Cause: Brake cables can break and hydraulic hoses pulled out in a crash.
Prevention: Use quality cables and replace them regularly.
Trail fix: Carry spare cables, one for the brakes and one for the gears. There's not much you can do about a failed hydraulic hose, though. Ride carefully home with the remaining brake.

8 FREEWHEEL FAILURE

Cause: Broken pawls in the freehub/ cassette body.

Prevention: Regular servicing and replacement, if necessary.

Trail fix: Secure the cassette to the spokes with zip ties and you can ride home with a crudely fixed gear.

9 REAR DERAILLEUR FAILURE

Cause: The derailleur can get stuck in the spokes and break, or get damaged after a crash.

Prevention: Check that the rear derailleur is straight and correctly adjusted.

Trail fix: Remove the rear derailleur and go "singlespeed."

10 CHAIN STUCK

Cause: Either worn chainrings or chain. The chain can get trapped onto the chainring and jammed into the frame.

Prevention: Replace worn chainring and/ or chain.

Trail fix: Try to use the big chainring to get home.

OTHER POTENTIAL PROBLEMS

THE CRANKS SNAP OR LOOSEN

Heavily used cranks may eventually break from fatigue – cracks usually appear first, so keep a close eye on them. Modern two-piece cranks are less prone to loosening than square taper units, but it can still happen. Whatever the style of crank, don't keep riding if they're loose – they'll be ruined quite quickly. Carry the correct size Allen wrench or wrench to fit the bolts.

THE PEDALS GET SMASHED OR FALL OFF

It is possible to ride with one foot, but it is a bit uncomfortable. If the pedal spindle is still intact you could try riding on that. Or wedge a suitably-sized stick in the pedal thread – don't expect it to take much weight, but it might be slightly better than nothing.

THE STEM SNAPS OR BENDS

This is rare, and there's not much you can do about it after it's happened. Don't attempt to ride a bent or cracked stem, and if you notice it failing during a ride then find some other way to get home. Munching the broken end of a stem is highly uncomfortable.

THE BARS SNAP OR BEND

You can get home using just one side of the bar if you shift it through the stem and just use one brake lever, but you won't be able to go far. Bent bars are just waiting to snap, so if you have a bad crash and they get bent replace them.

SEATPOST FAILURE

Seatpost breakages can be caused by fatigue or crashes. Check the post regularly with a straight edge – if it's bent, replace it. If your saddle comes off on a ride you'll have to ride out standing up.

THE HEADSET LOOSENS

Headsets can occasionally come loose, leading to a knocking sound and sensation from the front end. This should be tackled immediately to avoid damaging the bearings – threadless headsets usually just need a simple Allen wrench tweak (see page 110).

THE FRAME SNAPS

Time to walk home. Don't try to get creative with coat hangers or sticky, just plan your letter to the warranty department and call a taxi. Riding broken frames will be very dangerous, possibly fatal, so don't try it. Bent frames are just waiting to snap, so if your frame looks like it's bent get it checked out by a mechanic or frame builder.

BUCKLED WHEEL

If the buckle is incurable with a spoke wrench, try standing on it and get one of your riding buddies to stand on the other side of the buckle. Then you can jump up and down on the other side. This is a last resort – the wheel may pop back into shape, but this will probably ruin the rim and the spokes.

FORK FAILURE

A broken fork usually leads to a sudden and severe crash. Inspect forks regularly for any cracks, bends or suspicious discoloring. Steerer tube failures tend to occur where the tube joins the crown. This area can only be inspected by removing the fork. Suspension forks can fail internally, either losing air pressure or damping. If the fork won't hold air you can use the lockout lever (if present) to hold it up. Loss of damping will mean a very bouncy fork that you can only ride slowly on, but it'll get you home.

BRAKE PAD FAILURE

With regular checking you shouldn't wear out brake pads mid-ride, but some combinations of soil type, weather conditions and pad compound don't mix happily. Many riders have been caught out by premature pad failure. Fortunately pads are small, easy to carry and easy to install, so take a couple of spare sets with you just in case.

FULL SUSPENSION FAILURES

These depend very much on how severe the failure is. If the frame fails then it's very dangerous to ride it. If the shock fails you can usually ride home without too many problems, but you risk damaging the suspension unit or the frame so take it easy.

THE CHAINRING BENDS

The chainring can usually be bent back with some gentle persuasion (a big rock) or with a pair of pliers. A chainring tooth will break off quite easily, however, so don't force it.

TRANSPORTING YOUR BIKE

Most people don't have great riding from their doorstep, so it's likely that at some point you'll need to take your bike somewhere by car. There are several options for transporting your bike, each with advantages and disadvantages.

The safest way to carry your bike is in the back of your car. First, remove both the wheels (see pages 80-84). If you have hydraulic disc brakes, place a spacer between the pads just in case you activate the levers when placing your bike in the trunk. Wrap the chain and rear derailleur in a cloth so as not to get oil all over the place.

Try to pack your bike last and on top of (or alongside if your car permits) all your other equipment and lay the wheels under the frame. It's a good idea to get some wheel bags (trash bags are good too), especially if it's been muddy or wet. Try not to let the tires rub on anything sharp or you'll have a nasty shock when the sidewalls puncture.

ON A ROOF RACK

Remove all loose-fitting equipment, such as drink bottles, tool packs, pumps and so on. There are various styles of roof rack, but whichever it is make sure all the clamps and straps are fastened and give the bike a good shake to make sure it's secure. Before you drive off, double-check that all the straps are tight and you haven't left anything on the ground around the car or on top of the roof.

If you stop for anything, lock the bikes to the rack (most racks now have lockable fork fastenings) and always use a roof rack with lockable roof brackets. Lastly, don't go into a parking garage as this will ruin your bike, car and roof rack. And yes, it does happen more often than you might think!

ON A REAR RACK

Racks that strap on to the trunk lid are inexpensive and hence popular, but you have to be careful not to damage the car and they can be awkward to fit and load securely. You may also need to add a license plate if the one on the car is obscured. The best type of rack is one that attaches to a tow bar and supports the bikes by the wheels. We've attached tow bars to cars just to be able to use such a rack. Most tow bars can take the weight of a rack and three bikes, and those on larger cars will take four. Just be aware that the rack sticks out behind the car quite a long way.

PACKING YOUR BIKE

If you're flying with a bike, you'll need to pack it safely and securely. We have successfully flown with unpacked bikes with just the bars turned, but most airlines insist on them being boxed or bagged. Hard cases offer the best protection in transit, but they're expensive and heavy. Padded bags are cheaper, lighter and less likely to incur excess baggage charges but you need to pack them carefully to ensure your bike arrives safe and sound. The cheapest option of all is a big cardboard box like the ones bikes are delivered to shops in. Shops usually have to pay to get rid of these, so you can usually get one for free if you ask nicely. Add plenty of bubble wrap and tape.

1 Remove the wheels and take out the quick-release skewers. Even though luggage holds are pressurized, airlines still want tires and suspension units to be deflated. Leave a little air in the tires just to protect the rims and to provide some more padding. Place the wheels in the bag and tape them to one another, or use electrical zip ties. Space them so that the cassette and axle will not damage the frame. Cover the ends of the axle with cardboard to prevent them causing any damage inside the bag.

2 Remove the handlebars (whether or not you have to do this will depend on the type of bag you are using). If you are packing your bike in a bike box, you may well have to remove the bars to fold the bike flat. If you do, tighten the bolts that you have removed to prevent losing them and wrap the bars in bubble wrap. Tape anything like this in place with duct tape as it will damage your paint and ruin components if it rattles around. Use plenty of pipe insulation to protect the frame and around the suspension forks and the cranks too, as it absorbs a lot of shock. Lastly, don't forget to pack your pump, tools and, most importantly, a pedal wrench.

3 Remove the rear derailleur. This is worth doing as it's vulnerable and is one less thing to be sticking out and risk getting bent as your bike is thrown into the hold. Wrap it up in a plastic bag along with the chain. Duct tape it to the rear triangle, safely out of the way.

Rear Shock
Shock linkage
Shifters
Stem
Headset
Spokes
Tire
Hub
Rim
Brake caliper
Disc rotor
Brake levers
Suspension fork

Grips
Handlebars
Head tube
Brake hose
Gear cables
Front derailleur
Pedals
Crank arms
Rear derailleur
Saddle
Seatpost
Seat clamp

GLOSSARY

Items in italics denote another glossary entry.

29er: A bike with 29in wheels rather than the long-established 26in standard. Bigger wheels roll more easily over bumps, but add a little weight and can make bike fit awkward for shorter riders.

650B: Wheel size that sits between 26 and 29in. Rolls better than 26in but easier to package into full suspension or small hardtail frames than 29in.

Adjustable cup: Cartridge-style bottom bracket units usually have one fixed cup that's permanently attached to the bearing sleeve, and one adjustable cup that's wound in to align the unit in the frame.

Aheadset: Trade name for Dia-Compe's original design of threadless headset, now often used as a generic term for all such headsets.

Air spring: Suspension spring using compressed air. Lighter and easier to adjust than a coil spring, but needs more maintenance.

Bar end: Bolt-on handlebar extension providing an alternative hand position for climbing.

Bottom bracket: The axle and bearing assembly on which the crankarms rotate. The part of the frame into which the bottom bracket fits is called the bottom bracket shell.

Bradawl: A pointed tool designed for making pilot holes for screws. Useful for opening out the ends of freshly-cut cable housing.

Braze-on: Any frame fitting, including those for mounting cables, bottle cages, racks and so on. Such fittings are only actually brazed on to steel frames, but they're still called that even if welded, glued or riveted in place.

Bushing: a rotating bearing without balls or rollers, often used in rear suspension pivots.

Butting: A process used on steel, titanium or aluminum tubes whereby the ends are drawn thicker for strength at stress or weld points. The middle section of the tubes can be made thinner and therefore lighter as they are under less stress. Spokes can also be butted to save weight.

Cable puller: A plier-like tool that pulls a brake cable tight while pushing against the brake arm, making cable adjustment a two-, rather than three-handed job.

Cassette: A stack of sprockets that slides onto a splined *freehub*. This design replaced the screw-on freewheel – by integrating the freewheel mechanism into the hub rather than the sprockets, the hub bearings can be placed farther apart for strength. Cassette sprockets are also much easier to remove than threaded freewheels. Most modern MTBs now have 10-speed cassettes, although 9, 8 and 7 speed parts are still readily available.

Cantilever brake: Traditional *rim brake* design using two pivoting arms joined by a straddle cable. Lightweight, simple and reliable, but trickier to adjust than a V-brake.

Cartridge bearing: Self-contained, sealed unit comprising inner and outer races and ball bearings. Unlike *cup and cone bearings*, cartridge bearings are generally replaced rather than serviced.

Cassette lock ring: Threaded fitting used to secure a *cassette* to a *freehub*. Requires a specific splined tool to fit or remove.

Chain checker: Gauge to assess how worn a chain is. Worn chains lead to faster wear on sprockets and chainrings, so replacing them can save a big parts bill.

Chainline: The alignment of the chainrings and rear sprockets. The ideal chainline puts the middle chainring exactly in line with the center of the cassette, although the current standard MTB chainline puts the chainrings slightly farther out to accommodate large frame tubes.

Chainline gauge: Tool for checking *chainline*.

Chain slap: The annoying sound of the chain tap-dancing on your chainstay paintwork, usually heard when travelling at speed over rough ground. Chain slap may be due to a chain that's too long.

Chain suck: When the chain sticks to the chainring and is pulled up into the gap between chainring and frame. If it gets wedged you'll stop suddenly and the frame may be damaged. Usually the result of worn or dirty transmission components.

Chain whip: Tool used to hold the cassette still while the *lockring* is undone. If the *cassette* isn't held it'll just spin on the *freehub* when you attempt to undo the lockring.

Chromoly: Generic term for a range of light, strong steel alloys that include chromium and molybdenum in their constituents.

Cleats: Shaped metal plates bolted to the underside of riding shoes that engage in *clipless* pedals.

Clutch mech: Rear derailleurs that include a mechanism to slow down the fore-aft movement of the cage to reduce *chain slap*. Called Shadow Plus by Shimano and Type Two by SRAM.

Coil spring: Wound spring made of steel or titanium, used in some suspension forks and rear shocks, especially those intended for extreme riding. Coil springs are reliable and robust, but have limited adjustability and are much heavier than *air springs*.

Compatibility: Before index shifting, there was a period in mountain bike history when everything worked with everything else to at least some degree. Today some parts are interchangeable between brands but not all – a SRAM 10 speed cassette will work fine in an otherwise Shimano-based transmission, but a SRAM rear shifter won't correctly operate a Shimano rear mech (or vice versa).

Cone spanners: Thin spanners used to access the adjustable cones on hubs with *cup and cone bearings*.

Cranks: The arms, usually aluminum, that transfer your pedalling efforts to the chainrings. The cranks are just the arms themselves – cranks with chainrings fitted are referred to as a chainset.

Crank-removing tool: Threaded tool used to pull cranks from bottom bracket axles. Only used on *square taper, Octalink, ISIS* and similar designs.

Crown race remover: Bladed tool used to drift the bottom *headset* race off the fork *steerer tube*.

Crown race setting tool: Tubular tool for fitting the bottom *headset* race to the fork *steerer tube*. The race needs to be a tight fit, hence the need for a tool.

Cup and cone bearings: Bearings that use loose balls and adjustable bearing surfaces. Still often found in hubs.

Damper: Oil-filled chamber containing a piston to slow down the movement of a suspension fork or shock. Rebound damping controls the speed at which the unit extends to full length; compression damping controls the speed at which it compresses over bumps.

Derailleur: A French invention, perfected by Shimano, which shifts the chain across the chainrings and sprockets. Also known as a mech.

Disc brakes: Brakes that use a small hub-mounted rotor rather than the wheel rim as a braking surface. Disc brakes are now standard on mountain bikes, with only the very cheapest bikes using rim brakes.

Disc brake bleed kit: Collection of plastic tubes and syringes used to top up or replace the fluid in hydraulic brakes.

Drivetrain: Term for the whole transmission of the bike, from pedals to rear hub.

Eyeletted rims: Reinforcing eyelets are used around the spoke holes in a rim to spread the nipple tension and build a stronger wheel.

Facing: Process of removing excess material from the frame to ensure correct alignment of components. Head tubes, bottom bracket shells and brake mounts should all be faced.

Ferrules: The metal or plastic caps used to finish the ends of gear and brake cable housing.

Flat bar: Handlebar with the ends at the same height as the center, with just a gentle sweep between the two. Contrast with *riser bar*, which has the ends offset upwards relative to the center.

Flange: The section of the wheel hub into which the spokes hook.

Flats: Pedals with a large, spiked platform used in combination with flat-soled shoes. Once the preserve of downhill riders and dirt jumpers, flats are increasingly popular for all-round riding too.

Forging: A manufacturing process for components and frame parts, essentially involving hammering a lump of metal into shape. The resulting part is very strong.

Frame: The central and main component of the bike, to which all the other parts are mounted.

Freehub mechanism: The part of a rear hub that only allows the sprockets to rotate in one direction, thus allowing you to coast without turning the pedals.

Full suspension: A bike with suspension units at front and rear. Compare *hardtail* and *rigid*.

Geometry: The lengths and angles of the frame tubes that govern how a bike reacts to rider inputs. See *head angle*.

Granny gear: The smallest chainring, usually 22 teeth on a triple chainset. So called either because it's suitable for grannies to get up hills or simply because it doesn't have many teeth.

Gripshift: Twist shifter made by SRAM. Very light and simple, although most riders prefer trigger shifters.

Headset: The bearings that allow the fork to turn in the frame to facilitate steering.

Headset cup remover: Rocket-shaped tool for hammering *headset* cups out of the frame.

Headset press: Threaded tool used to push *headset* cups into the frame.

Housing: The flexible outer casings that guide gear and brake cables along the frame. Gear housing is made using longitudinal steel strands so that it doesn't compress, allowing for accurate *indexing*.

Hubs: The rotating element at the center of the wheel. May use either *cup and cone* or *cartridge* bearings. If *disc brakes* are used, the brake rotor will be mounted to the hub.

Indexing: Gear system with shift levers that click once for each gear, making shifting easier.

Jockey wheels: Pair of small sprockets in the *rear derailleur* mounted in a sprung, pivoting cage that controls chain tension.

Machined rims: Rims are made from a strip of alloy, so have to be joined to form a circle. Machining the sidewalls of the rim ensures that there's no step at the join, giving smoother braking.

PCD: Pitch Circle Diameter, the distance between the fixing bolts on chainrings.

Pivot point: where the suspension lever pivots. The farther forward the pivot point, the plusher the suspension will be in the saddle (and firmer out of it). When the rider is seated there is greater leverage on the pivot point and hence the shock. As the rider stands the weight moves forward, thereby lessening the leverage and un-weighting the shock.

Plain gauge: Frame tubes that have the same wall thickness along their length, as opposed to butted tubes, which are thicker at the ends than in the center. Can also refer to spokes.

Rapidfire: Shimano's name for its twin-lever trigger shifters – press one lever to shift up, the other lever to shift down.

Rapid Rise: Also known as "Low Normal," an ill-fated Shimano design that sprung the *rear derailleur* towards the large sprocket rather than the small one, reversing the action of the shifter.

Rear derailleur: See *rear mech.*

Rear shock: See *Shock.*

Remote lockout: Bar-mounted lever to lock the front or rear suspension to prevent it moving on smooth ground.

Replaceable hanger: The part of the frame to which the *rear derailleur* bolts is vulnerable to damage in a crash. On steel frames it can be bent back, but aluminum and carbon frames usually have bolt-on hangers that are easily replaced.

Rigid fork: Front fork with fixed legs, rather than a telescopic suspension fork. Unusual on new bikes but by no means extinct.

Rim brake: Brake that acts on the wheel rim to slow the bike.

Riser bars: Handlebars with a double bend to offset the grips upwards from the stem, giving a higher riding position.

Rocket tool: See *Headset cup remover.*

Sag: the amount the suspension compresses as you simply sit on the bike.

Shock: Spring/damper unit used to suspend the back end of the bike.

Singletrack: A trail just wide enough for one bike. The most popular kind of trail to ride, especially if it has lots of corners.

Sliders: The lower legs of a suspension fork that move up and down on the stanchions.

Spider: The part of the crank that attaches the chainrings to the cranks.

Spoke tension meter: Device for measuring how tight the spokes of a wheel are. Spoke tensions need to be even for a long-lasting wheel.

Sprockets: The toothed wheels at the back of the bike with which the chain engages to drive the rear wheel.

Stanchion: The fixed legs of a suspension fork, along which the lower legs slide up and down.

Star-fangled nut: Spiked nut that fits into the top of the fork and has the headset top cap threaded into it. Tightening the top cap increases the preload on the headset bearings to eliminate play.

Stiction: Contraction of static friction, the resistance to initial movement of a suspension fork or shock due to seal drag.

Top-out: A knocking caused by the suspension rebounding too quickly due to insufficient damping or too high a spring rate. Some budget suspension forks top out however they're adjusted. Using all the suspension travel is known as "bottoming out."

Tubeless tires: Tires with a special locking bead designed to work without inner tubes, making pinch punctures less likely and allowing lower tire pressures for better grip.

INDEX

Mike Davis and Guy Andrews

the roadside MOUNTAIN BIKE maintenance manual

FALCON GUIDES®

GUILFORD, CONNECTICUT
HELENA, MONTANA

AN IMPRINT OF GLOBE PEQUOT PRESS

Note

While every effort has been made to ensure that the content of this book is as technically accurate and as sound as possible, neither the author nor the publishers can accept responsibility for any injury or loss sustained as a result of the use of this material.

First edition 2014 published by Bloomsbury Publishing Plc
50 Bedford Square
London WC1B 3DP
www.bloomsbury.com

This American edition of The Roadside Mountain Bike Maintenance Manual, First Edition, is published by Globe Pequot Press by arrangement with Bloomsbury Publishing Plc.
First Globe Pequot Press edition 2014.

FalconGuides is an imprint of Globe Pequot Press
Falcon, FalconGuides and Outfit Your Mind are registered trademarks of Morris Book Publishing LLC.

Guy Andrews and Mike Davis have asserted their rights under the Copyright, Design and Patents Act, 1988, to be identified as the authors of this work.

Library of Congress Cataloging-in-Publication data is available on file.
ISBN 978-0-7627-9692-2

Cover photographs © Gerard Brown
Inside photographs © Gerard Brown
Designed by Jonathan Briggs

This book is produced using paper that i
sustainable forests. It is natural, renewab
The logging and manufacturing processe of
the country of origin.

Printed in China by South China Printing
10 9 8 7 6 5 4 3 2 1